- # Because I Think,
    I Believe

A Personal Christian Manifesto

Copyright © Donald R. Wilson, 2010. All rights reserved. No part of this book may be reproduced or transmitted in any form or by any means, electronic or mechanical, including photocopying, recording, or by any information storage and retrieval system, without permission in writing from the publisher.

Millennial Mind Publishing
An imprint of American Book Publishing
5442 So. 900 East, #146
Salt Lake City, UT 84117-7204
www.american-book.com
Printed in the United States of America on acid-free paper.

Because I Think, I Believe
Designed by Jana Rade, design@american-book.com

Publisher's Note: American Book Publishing relies on the author's integrity of research and attribution; each statement has not been investigated to determine if it has been accurately made. The author and publisher specifically disclaim any responsibility for any liability, loss, or risk, personal or otherwise, which is incurred as a consequence, directly or indirectly, of the use and application of any of the contents of this book. In such situations where medical, legal, or other professional services may apply, please seek the advice of such professionals directly.

ISBN-13: 978-1-58982-754-7
ISBN-10: 1-58982-754-6

Library of Congress Cataloging-in-Publication Data

Wilson, Donald R.
  Because I think, I believe : a personal Christian manifesto / Donald R. Wilson.
     p. cm.
  Includes bibliographical references (p.   ).
  ISBN-13: 978-1-58982-754-7
  ISBN-10: 1-58982-754-6
  1. Apologetics. 2. Faith and reason--Christianity. I. Title.
  BT1212.W55 2010
  239'.7--dc22
                                2010024303

Special Sales: These books are available at special discounts for bulk purchases. Special editions, including personalized covers, excerpts of existing books, and corporate imprints, can be created in large quantities for special needs. For more information e-mail info@american-book.com.

• Because I Think,
I Believe

A Personal Christian Manifesto

Donald R. Wilson

Contents

Introduction 1
   The Impact of Evolution... 3
   A Logical Belief System 7
   The Testimony of an Ordinary Person 9

Chapter One
What Do We Really Know about Anything? 13
   Fundamental Truth—The Elephant in the Room 13
   The Problem of Finding Truth 16
   Science as the Source of All Truth 19
   Post-Modern Ideas 21
   All Knowledge Is Based on Faith in our Assumptions 23
   We All Have Faith in a Non-Physical Reality 30
   The Human Need for Meaning 32
   Right and Wrong, Good and Bad 33
   Can Anything Be Known Unquestionably? 35

Chapter Two
Who Are We and Why Are We Here? 37
   Specified Complexity 38
   The Real "You" 39
   The Internal Moral Yardstick 41
   The Basic Attributes of God 46

    For Your Information 48
    Mankind's Persistent Arrogance 51
    The Blessing, and Curse, of Curiosity 52
    The Purpose of Our Existence 54

Chapter Three
What Is Christianity Anyway? 57
    Religion versus Christianity 57
    The Importance of Transcendent Truth 59
    Christianity versus Secular Humanism 63
    Attacks That Miss the Mark 65
    Finding the Right Path to Truth 66
    The Role of Faith 67
    The Spiritual Realm 72
    The Freedom to Choose 72

Chapter Four
Who Is God, and Why Do So Many Disagree about Him? 75
    The Only Accurate History of the Ancient World 77
    The Effects of the Great Flood 79
    The Scattering of Mankind Over the Earth 81
    The Apparent Primitiveness of Early Man 82
    The Origin of Conflicting Religions 84
    It Could Have Been Different 86
    A Modern Resurgence of a Universal Need 88
    The Nature of the Christian God 90

Chapter Five
Why Can the Christian Bible Be Trusted over Other Religious Writings? 93
    The Bible's Secular Reputation 95
    An Amazing Book 96

The Verification of Science and History............................99
The Verification of Prophecy 102
What about Other Religious Texts?..............................106
The Apocrypha 107
The Implications of the Bible's Teachings 110

Chapter Six
Why Does God Seem So Angry and Sometimes Even Cruel?...113
The Wrath of God..114
Who We're Dealing With 115
Judging God 117
Not So Bad After All 118
The Creator Owns His Creation 120
There Is Always a Reason 122
God's Unmerited Mercy...124
Is God Apathetic?..125
Who Is Responsible for Evil in the World? 129
The Reason We Are Separated from God................130
Why Such an Awful Place as Hell? 133
The Means of Reconciliation 135

Chapter Seven
If God Is Real, Why Is Jesus the Only Way to Him?...................................139
The Claims of Christ...140
The Atheist Mindset..142
Christ's Fulfillment of Prophecy 143
The Historical Validity of the Resurrection.............145
The "Swoon Theory"...147
The Conspiracy Theory 149
Other Weak and Wishful Explanations 153
The Critical Importance of the Resurrection 155

Chapter Eight
**What Makes Christians
So Sure They Have It Right?** **161**
   The Power, and the Impotence, of Apologetics 162
   The Final Piece of the Truth Puzzle 164

Chapter Nine
What about This, and What about That? **171**
   A Few Sticking Points 173
   The Authority of Scripture 174
   The Exclusivity of the Christian Claim to Truth 175
   Historical Science and the Bible 176
   The "D" Word 181
   The Absolute Criticality of Accepting
   the Plain Meaning of Genesis 182
   On the Other Hand… 187
   Does Attacking Christians
   Really Discredit Christianity? 189
   A Restriction to Freedom? 194
Appendix **199**
Suggested Reading **205**
Acknowledgment **209**
About the Author **211**

This book is dedicated to

*Ryan, Lindsey, Adam, Lauren, Cookie, Merrill,
Paul, Danielle, Jason, Michael*

*And above all,
Debbie,
my rescuer, who enabled me
to grow enough to write this book.*

*With special thanks to the late
Charlotte Kusche,
because the work of her life is in this book.*

Introduction

"To you I'm an atheist.
To God, I'm the loyal opposition."
—*Woody Allen*

A while back, I met a young man. Better put, I became reacquainted with a young man whom I used to know. I'll call him James. When I knew James well, he was a boy, but this time I had the opportunity to know him as a man, and he had changed a lot from the boy I knew before. As a boy, James was a sweet kid—one of those whom everybody wants to hug at first sight. He was curly-haired, compliant, compassionate, and likable. Not much of that has changed.

Throughout his childhood and well into adolescence and early manhood, James had fully embraced the Christian world view taught to him by his family. By the time I was reacquainted with him, though, he had become what he described as a humanist-atheist, having rejected completely the faith of his parents. Like most who describe themselves similarly, he was reluctant to discuss his beliefs because his experience had been that such discussions quickly turn into sermons served up by the opposing side. He was sick and tired of what he saw as meaningless attempts at piety and the bombardments of predictable rhetoric that would be poured upon him by the religious faithful, whom he rarely saw as faithful at all when he looked at the witness of their lives. If you feel similarly, this book is written for you.

Eventually though, James did agree to exchange views with me on the basis of reasoning rather than declarations of religious faith, and because I realized that his life experiences had disillusioned him about the idea of any kind of faith at all, this was okay with me. The rules of engagement were set. James was a guy who felt that he had given faith (or in my understanding of him, *religion*) a full chance in his life and had found, in the end, no substance to it. Further, he seemed certain there was no supernatural, no reality outside of what could be seen or otherwise experienced by the human senses, or if there was such a supernatural reality, there was no way we could know or experience it. He is an intelligent debater, well informed on science issues and consistent in his reasoning, and he defended his positions fiercely. At first, I enjoyed the discussions because his bright mind seemed open to ideas and his debate skills challenged me to present as well-reasoned or demonstrable arguments as I could muster. So I pursued the discourse with him, mostly by e-mail exchanges, and I began praying for his mind to remain open and insight and enlightenment to descend on him.

At that time, at least, it was not to be so. After a number of intense exchanges, I began to realize that James' position was galvanized to the point that, barring a significant breakthrough in his life, he was probably unreachable, at least by any persuasion that I might be capable of. Moreover, the argument had gotten a little contentious, so I chose to end the discussions.

I've met others like James in my life. Some have been open and seemed reachable with enough time and persuasion, but my experience has been that many are not. Rather, they seem to be, as the scripture puts it, "*given up to … the lusts of their own hearts, [because they have] changed the truth of God into a lie, and worshipped and served the [created] more than the Creator,*"[1] and it would seem that only the Creator God Himself, should He choose to violate their free choice, could be able to reach them. It always makes me sad when I come to realize this about a person. But in James' case, I was more than sad, because he is someone I love.

The Impact of Evolution

As the Western world becomes more and more secularized, an ever larger portion of the population is moving toward believing what James believes—that they are nothing but the product of colossal cosmic accidents over eons followed by more eons of chaotic, impossibly unlikely, chance chemical occurrences.

Who can blame them, really, when they have been bombarded relentlessly throughout their formative years with this idea from virtually all quarters? Few realize the full implications of this, Christians and other religious people included. Not only are the truths presented in the Bible categorically rejected, even ridiculed, by a society that holds them in contempt, but these truths are becoming increasingly disconnected from Christianity's view of the world as well. In our society today, few know what to believe with regard to their origin and the true nature of their reality. Because intelligent people with common sense find problems with every world view available, it seems that philosophers, clerics, scientists, and laymen alike find no completely rational, foundational belief system on which to stand. And because no one ever uncovers a truly sound explanation for the world in which they find themselves, I believe they often resort to one of these three approaches to the problem:

---

[1] Romans 1:24, 25. Brackets are author's; meaning is not changed. This is the case wherever brackets are included in Bible quotations herein.

Introduction

1. They adopt whatever sounds good to them at first hearing (sometimes changing it when they think they hear something better).
2. They adopt what strong leaders and other life-influencers have believed (meaning, sometimes, what the majority of their peers believe).
3. They try never to think about what they believe (in fact, they insist upon never thinking about it!).

The last option is becoming more and more prevalent, in my experience. It is profoundly odd to me that the human race is so fond of truth in all of the objective areas of life, yet most people insist upon being utterly disinterested in whatever transcendent, foundational truth underlies their existence. There are reasons for this phenomenon that I hope will become clear in the pages that follow.

But among those who will at least contemplate the meaning of their existence, humanism, materialism, naturalism[2] and their various nuances seem to be making great inroads. This, I believe, is largely because the teaching of evolution and various other forms of random-chance origins theory have become some of the most influential "leaders" people experience during their lives. Such theories have led a great many in our society to believe they can depend on science to

> *Even those who are not religious are beginning to declare that there must have been some kind of an intelligent designer.*

---

[2] Although there are differences between these terms, they are all based on atheism, and basically imply a rejection of any spiritual reality. For simplicity, I will use them interchangeably throughout this book.

find and share with the masses the answers to every question. And sadly, it has led a large percentage of those who would call themselves Christian to allow "science" to pass judgment on the truths of scripture as well.

Because they believe so wholeheartedly in science's ability to reveal the truth about unrecorded history, many people logically conclude, based on what secular science is telling them, that there is no reason to believe in God. Though some do believe in some kind of spiritual plane, a large number believe that this physical existence, however long it lasts, is all there will be. I don't blame them at all for reaching this kind of conclusion. It is a perfectly logical one derived from the vast majority of what they've been taught (whether they were brought up in a religious setting or not).

If you are into labels, this way of viewing the world is dubbed "modern" by philosophers. It is a "modernist" point of view, and its roots are firmly planted in Darwinism.[3]

I believe that one of the critical answers to this rabid societal error is to break down the massive monolith of evolution in the shadow of which we all live. Fortunately, many brilliant professionals are now busy doing that, and more are joining the chorus all the time. Ph.D. scientists as well as outstanding clergymen and laymen are speaking out against this inane theory, making the strong case that it in no way stands up to the light of true inquiry. Even those who are not religious are beginning to courageously declare that there must have been some kind of an intelligent designer, although they often suffer damage to their careers just for saying it. There is no other answer that truly comports with reason. If one accepts Darwinism, it's perfectly reasonable to reject God. But

---

[3] It will be noted later that modernism is being rapidly displaced by "post-modernism," which denies all forms of objective truth, recognizing that there is likely a supernatural world but claiming no ability to know it.

Introduction

if reason is the goal, then questioning Darwinism is a must.

Another potential treatment for this pervasive cancer lies in a needed fundamental change in the approach the Christian church takes to teaching its people and reaching unbelievers. There is something missing in our education as we mature in this world. In fact, it is a cavernous, truth-sized hole in the structure upon which we build our understanding of reality. From schooling, we get a thorough indoctrination in physical science, mathematics and the like, and we are taught to read and understand some of what wise or gifted men and women have written before us. From church, if we go, we hear truth-claims about another side of life—the spiritual side. The trouble is, what we hear in school often directly contradicts what we hear in church. Our school curricula are very thorough about laying out detailed reasons why we should believe what we are being told, and these reasons seem to be backed up by the most vocal of our cultural influencers. Famous scientists with multiple degrees and published works are quoted, and our teachers, even those who don't really agree, compliantly support these "facts." But in church, we hear only claims, usually from an ancient book or from someone's personal experience. We almost never hear detailed academic reasons why these church claims should be believed. The spiritual declarations heard in church can be powerful, it's true, and they can evoke emotional responses and make us want dearly to believe them. But these responses are fleeting, because lurking outside the church doors is always "reality." The hard facts, we think. And eventually we are won over by them.

Whether you believe it or not, there exists a valid body of thought—an academically rigorous set of arguments—that contradicts much of what the secular world is teaching us. These arguments stand up to the demands of logical, philosophical, and scientific reasoning as well as anything in, say, any biology textbook. As a matter of fact, one finds that the reasoning in any accepted biology textbook regarding "evolutionary biology" is arbitrary and inconsistent. Many times it is even laughable. But where are we to go to hear this other point of view so that we can make a reasoned evaluation for ourselves? Society prevents us from hearing it in school, and it is never systematically laid out for us in church. Unless our parents teach us, or we are interested enough in thorough inquiry to dig into it for ourselves, we are barely aware of its existence. So we are susceptible to believing secular claims that there is no evidence supporting creation or refuting evolution. This needs to change if the church is to remain a meaningful influence on our society, and I call upon any church leader reading these words to be a catalyst for change in this area.

A Logical Belief System

But these are not really my purposes in writing this manifesto, as I call it. I am not a scientist, nor highly qualified to refute evolutionary theories, though I am well read on the subject. Because of the complicated scientific and historical issues involved, I won't try to make a detailed case that neo-Darwinism is the wishful thinking of those who want desperately to explain all they see in strictly materialist terms, though I believe that to be the case. But the issue is fundamental to my argument, so you will find it woven throughout the book. I touch on some specific points in my last chapter.

Much of what many skeptics believe about Christianity is based on misunderstanding.

Nor am I in much of a position to effect a change in the way the church approaches teaching its people. What I am is simply a person—a Christian—doing in a formal way what I think all Christians are called to do—to *"give a reason for the hope that is within* [me] *with gentleness and respect."*[4] If you are a skeptic, I have no "quarrel" with you, and my intent is to respect you and your right to believe what you believe. You are endowed with that right by your Creator. I just don't happen to agree with you. I read a lot of views that oppose mine, and I hope that by doing that, I can better understand those who disagree with me.

What I want to do herein is to declare the *logic* of a belief in God and the Christian faith and to point out some of the logical difficulties of trying to avoid such a belief. I know from my conversations with them that most atheists and agnostics will not take spiritual or experiential arguments seriously. They have already chosen to reject them as mere sentimental manipulation. Telling convinced atheists about what your faith has meant to you or that God loves them usually has little impact, I've found, because they haven't experienced those things for themselves. With those who have already made a philosophical commitment to materialism, such talk is just emotionalism and wishful thinking. Many of them consider themselves intellectuals (not to imply that they aren't), and they want to compare reason to reason and leave emotionalism out of it. If you are one of these, then I say, "Fair enough."[5]

Much of what many skeptics believe about Christianity is based on misunderstanding, and my hope is to set the record somewhat straight, at least for some, regarding what Christianity is and what it is not and to provide a logical basis for faith in

---

[4] I Peter 3:15.
[5] Note that I am not saying that I'm willing to meet my opponents on "neutral ground." There is no such thing as neutral ground in this discussion. Atheists and others have fundamental beliefs based on their life's experiences, and so do I. We each have a right and an obligation to bring these presuppositions to the discussion and evaluate them.

The Creator, because I believe that it is only through faith in Him that we understand the permanence, value and meaning in each of our lives. If you are a skeptic who is still open to finding truth, I ask you to step back for a few hours from your doubts. A powerful atheist thinker, Bertrand Russell, said that to think freely is to free oneself from the tyranny of one's passions. Beliefs that we hold strongly do maintain a sort of tyrannical hold on us. But we shouldn't allow this to be the case unless and until we have satisfied ourselves that we have broken the hold of this tyranny and listened fairly, thoroughly and openly to opposing viewpoints often enough to be sure that our passions are justified. It is only then that we see the strength of reason behind our passions and become confident, reasoned believers in them. So I ask you to put your criticisms and the many things you've heard about Christianity on a safe shelf for a while and ask yourself honestly the questions raised in this book. You can plan to pick your criticisms up when you've finished reading.

And to Christians who read this, I hope you will be strengthened and confirmed in your faith. This book is as much for you as for doubters. Perhaps more so. Our faith is firmly grounded in logic and good evidence, and I hope that laying it out this way will increase your confidence and peace and give you some tools you might find useful in defending your faith.

The Testimony of an Ordinary Person

What follows are the perceptions of a long-time Christian who, like so many others, has stumbled and struggled for much of his lifetime with issues regarding the reasonableness and the import of his faith. It is the effort of one ordinary person to organize his thoughts about this most critical of issues and to offer them for the consideration of whoever might be willing to hear.

Every day, Christians and others who seek to understand

Introduction

Christianity are intimidated by the arrogant, dismissive bullying the secular world has dished out over the past century and more. I hope this book encourages a few of them that you don't need a Ph.D. to understand the issues in this war of world views.

This manifesto is intended to be focused on the core issues of Christianity, but there is a great deal more to discuss and to learn. Almost anyone who reads this book will soon begin saying, "What about this?" and "What about that?" (Hence, the title of the closing chapter.) Getting those answers is important to the extent that modern man understands enough to provide them. The recommended reading at the end of the book is selected partially with the intent of providing amplification on some matters not fully expanded in the text. I have read and been impressed by each one of them, and I encourage you to read them too. No matter what answers you may find, every person must first deal with what is said in this book in a way that settles for them the core question of which world view accurately explains reality. A decision must be made. There are no faith-free world views. Avoiding a decision is deciding by default. It is a requirement of your inborn curiosity, your need for meaning and purpose, *and it affects your future like no other matter.*

— Don Wilson

"For the time will come when people will not put up with sound doctrine. Instead, to suit their own desires, they will gather around them a great number of teachers to say what their itching ears want to hear. They will turn their ears away from the truth and turn aside to myths. But you [must] keep your head in all situations..."

—*Paul, the Apostle*

II Timothy 4:3-5
First century A.D.

Chapter One

What Do We Really Know about Anything?

"To know that we know what we know, and to know that we do not know what we do not know, that is true knowledge."
—*Copernicus*

Why is it that human beings are so different from each other in the things they believe and the way they think and act? Why do we have such strong disagreements about right and wrong and about what is valuable and worthless that at times we are able to slaughter each other by the hundreds of thousands in order to advance our cause or protect our perceived rights? If we are the same species, with DNA that some say varies by less than 0.2%, shouldn't we all understand life and our environment in a very similar way?

Fundamental Truth—The Elephant in the Room

A funny, though rather cynical, story crossed my path not long ago in which a naturalist photographer spent many months somewhere in the African wilderness photographing elephants in the wild. During the long months in and out of his blind, he had become interested in a particular young bull who seemed less shy of humans, or at least of the photographer, and who acted much less aggressively than the other bulls. At one point, as the elephant was reaching full maturity, the photographer decided to bravely approach him, and though he knew that the huge beast could kill him at its slightest whim, the photographer tentatively reached out and touched the animal on its foreleg. Giving the photographer a start at first, the elephant raised the leg, bent at the knee, and held it there. When the photographer recovered from his initial fright, he realized that the animal was holding the leg there as an invitation for him to touch it. So the photographer stroked the animal's leg and talked gently to it until it lost interest and turned away. This interaction was repeated in various ways over the time remaining, and the photographer and the elephant became great "friends." When he got home, the photographer told the story many times to his family, and he never forgot the young elephant.

Some years later, the man had occasion to take his son to the zoo, and being somewhat of an expert, he was anxious to reach the elephant enclosure and explain various interesting facts about them to his son. As they leaned against the railing and observed the animals, the man sort of "caught the eye" of one of the elephants. It was an adult male about the age that his African "friend" would have been by then, and it seemed to be looking directly at the two humans. As the man watched the elephant, he became convinced that it was the same individual, and more than that, he was sure the animal recognized him. Against all caution, the man made an impulsive decision. He carefully stepped over the railings and approached the friendly-looking creature, full of confidence that this was indeed his "friend." As he reached out his hand to touch the animal in the same familiar gesture from the African savannah, the elephant raised its foreleg…

… and stomped the man to death.

It probably wasn't the same elephant.

There's a lesson to be learned from this story (believe it or not) about the importance of finding truth on which to base our view of life. Truth of this kind is like a gentle elephant in a wild herd of violent and aggressive ones. It's hard to find, and if you choose unwisely, it can cost you your life!

With apologies for pressing the elephant analogies to the limit, a correct understanding of reality—or fundamental, transcendent truth—is also like the famous "elephant in the room," is it not? Each person who is mentally stable and healthy knows that his or her understanding of this kind of truth has the most far-reaching effect possible on how he or she views the world. Yet because getting to an understanding of the true nature of our reality seems so impossibly complex, many don't deal with it at all. It is that massive issue present in every "room" of a person's life that no one ever talks about or acknowledges is there. But there can be no doubt it is the most important knowledge we will ever pursue.

> *Truth…is like a gentle elephant in a wild herd of violent and aggressive ones. It's hard to find, and if you choose unwisely, it can cost you your life!*

What *is* the absolutely true character of the environment into which we have been born? Surely this environment can't be uniquely different for every person, or even for different groups of people. There must be some characteristics that describe it accurately for everyone. What are these characteristics? This question underlies all of our perceptions, and the way in which we answer it informs everything we believe and trust. It strongly influences our personalities and points of view. It shapes what we view as important, and it directs our values and choices. There can be nothing more important to the human psyche than finding this truth and having a firm belief in its categorical validity. It is the truth that lies beneath and supports all other truth. In fact, it's my belief that the ability to reach a confident understanding of the true nature of reality is the foundation of human psychological well-being. Finding it can heal and save our lives, and failing to find it can cause untold suffering. If we are wise, we will ignore the great social and emotional risks that go along with examining the elephant in the room and courageously search among the great herd of truth-claims, which is mostly made up of violent and aggressive error, for that one kind elephant that will make sense of our lives.

The Problem of Finding Truth

Enough about elephants.

When you start digging into truth, you find that in the human mind's own power, it turns out to be an incredibly difficult thing to judge. What does "the truth" even mean? The truth according to whom? According to one's government? One's family or peer group? Science? Religion? Any reasonably experienced adult knows that the so-called truth about anything can be different depending upon who you're asking.

There's legal truth. For instance, I'm told that it is legal for a purveyor of poultry to call his product "fresh" (i.e., not frozen) if it was never stored below 26°F. And he can legally use the description "never frozen" if it was never stored below 1°F! Does that legal authority make these claims "true"?[1] In another example, slavery was legal and African blacks had no right to citizenship, according to the Dred-Scott decision of 1857. Did

---

[1] This "fact" was related to me as hearsay, so I apologize to the reader if it is not factual. But it does make the point.

that make it true that slavery was acceptable and that people's inherent rights were different based on the concentration of melanin in their skin?

What about political truth? When a politician declares her alarm over poverty while at the same time working to perpetuate it because she sees the poor as her main constituency and wants to maintain it, is she telling the "truth"? Is it true that one political philosophy is better for a given nation than another? Which one, in what circumstance and who says so?

The same applies to knottiest of all subjects, moral truth. What is the real "truth" about what is right and what is wrong, or what is valuable and what is worthless? Is there such a truth? Humankind spends plenty of time arguing about this kind of truth.

As we'll see in the following pages, the business of truth-finding by limited human beings can be more difficult than fishing by hand. Each time you think you've gotten a truth cornered, it again proves too quick to catch or too slippery to hold. Usually, when two people are patient enough to discuss in depth the question of what is indisputably true in life, they end up, after a long back-and-forth, agreeing that the truth about life, the universe, morality, religion and how things really are is too great a thing for the human mind to fully grasp. At the end of the discussion, they often arrive at what they do and do not agree upon regarding foundational truth, but because they each see the world a little differently, they usually part convinced that, in the strictest sense, these are beliefs, not demonstrable facts.

> *Because we are unique in all of nature, we have the capacity and the need to ask questions.*

Part of the problem, of course, is that we are fitted with only a limited number of tools with which we can sense our environment. We see, touch, taste, smell, and feel the world around us, so as long as we don't question the validity of our sensory inputs or our brain's interpretation of them, we feel like we have a pretty good handle on at least the physical nature of our environment, its visible characteristics and how it relates to us. In this way we are not much different from the other creatures of the earth.

Reality, though, goes beyond what the five senses are able to perceive. The unfortunate thing (some might say), when it comes to this ultimate truth quest, is that we humans are also fitted with ways to test, question, and sense our environment that are unique only to us. And this is where we run into trouble. We have capacities we call reason, self-awareness, compassion and curiosity, among many others, coupled with intelligence greater by orders of magnitude than any other species with which we share our planet. Because we are unique in all of nature, we have the capacity and the need to ask questions. We realize it's possible that the input from our senses may be in error, that it may not tell the whole story or that others may perceive things differently than we do. We realize that there are limits to what our senses can perceive and to how well we process their input, so our curiosity drives us to ask ourselves whether there are elements of our reality that are outside these limits. These realizations, among many others, and the gifts from which they arise, are unique to our species. In short, we understand in a way no other creature could that the things upon which we base our understanding of truth are tentative and incomplete at best.

Philosopher Immanuel Kant (1724-1804), drawing on the ideas of Protagoras (490-420 BC), was the first to express the probability that man does not possess sufficient sensory apparatus to be certain he knows the truth about reality. Kant suggested that because we can only sense our environment with the limited tools given to us, we only know for certain what we *experience* about reality, not the nature of reality itself.[2] What if we sensed our environment in ways completely unknown to us? Isn't it possible, even probable, that we would understand it differently? Someone has said that a fish doesn't know it's wet. Can we be sure we know our environment any better?

This philosophical argument frustrated a lot of people in Kant's day, and it has the same effect on many today, because although we see the logic of it and have no real argument against it, it goes against our inner belief that there must be some way to arrive at an understanding of what things are unshakably true about our lives. We want to know that it's possible, if we struggle hard enough, to reach the truth about our most important issues. We're not satisfied with just giving up and admitting we don't know. This need is what drives us to wonder about what is really true concerning everything we encounter. Christianity suggests that we (all of us) are born with this inner need, that it drives us to find answers and gives us hope that one day we will fully understand. It's what makes us argue over aspects of truth proposed by others and seek to resolve them for ourselves. It's what makes us human.

But since there is so much disagreement about it, how in the world can we ever be certain we have gotten to this ultimate truth?

Science as the Source of all Truth

Absolute truth, or transcendent, unchanging truth, can be defined as that which corresponds to reality. But is physical reality the only reality that exists? In recent times, mankind has begun to experience some profound changes of mind about this

---

[2] See Immanuel Kant, *A Critique of Pure Reason*, first published in 1781.

question. Over the past couple of centuries, Western culture, especially, experienced an unparalleled ideological shift. A great many in the West and worldwide came to believe that science, in its various disciplines, would be capable of eventually providing mankind with all truth, that anything knowable can be seen and quantified and that if anything else exists (which some doubted), it is unknowable.[3]

This view was unprecedented historically. Until the past century and a half, the vast majority of the human species living in Western cultures believed that there is much inherent truth that originates from outside of what is available to our senses or provable in the scientific-method sense—that there is a truth which transcends nature and material things. This same view was held strongly by a very large majority in the United States until it began eroding during this period, chiefly because of Charles Darwin's ideas and the rapid advancement in the understanding of our natural world that has occurred concurrently. Discoveries about the physical world have made it possible for many to conclude that science will, and in most cases has, nailed down the mercurial answers to whatever questions of ultimate truth man is capable of knowing. Beginning even before the so-called Enlightenment, and spurred on by Darwin and others, the kidnapping of science by naturalist philosophers has been nearly completed. These philosophers, based on their distaste for the idea of a god and on the idea that science can find in nature an answer to every question, wish to explain the fundamental truths

The kidnapping of science by naturalist philosophers has been nearly completed.

---

[3] This belief, as indicated in the introduction, is known in philosophy as positivism and is a part of the philosophy of modernism.

of life without evoking or recognizing any entity or force outside of nature. Most scientific disciplines, in an end-justifies-the-means mentality, have sold rank speculation and wishful thinking to a trusting populace as science. Today, many still believe that nothing at all exists *but* that which is physical, or at least that whatever may lie outside of the material world is strange and separate from it.

Post-Modern Ideas

As I said, though—materialist marketing aside—most people[4] do realize in the backs of their minds that there are, in fact, things outside of the natural world that are real. They realize that truths about things like morals and values, for instance, don't lend themselves easily to analysis in the same way that purely physical things do. So in recent decades, it has become more and more popular to reject positivism in favor of a belief that we can't really know anything for sure (while, oddly, still holding firmly to Darwinism). Certainly, it's believed, one can't analyze moral questions and come up with factual answers applying to everyone, so the latest step in modern philosophy has been to teach that these things are so driven by culture and environment that there cannot be one truth discovered about them for all people in all circumstances. Truth, these people say, is relative to the culture and to the situation. Because of this, it is becoming a fundamental belief of many that truth is relative to each person's individual sensibilities and conscience.[5] You have an absolute right to "your own truth," and no one has a right to trump it with theirs. Of course, when you really think about it, this proposition is self-defeating. Wouldn't one be required to

---

[4] I would argue *all* people.
[5] This change in philosophy from positivism to relativism is known as post-modern.

know the *absolute* truth about life in order to claim dogmatically that such truth is *relative*?

This kind of confusion about how things really are is understandable and even inevitable in a society where the "powers that be" (media, science, academia, et al.) pursue an agenda designed to press their own materialist world view, a view which denies any kind of ultimate moral or legal authority. If the material world is all there is, then moral truth is indeed relative to individual or societal preferences, and the foundation of every person's morality becomes shifting sand.

Furthermore, if, as Darwinian evolution claims, our brains are formed by nature from those of lower animals, how can we trust any thoughts we may have about higher truth anyway? If natural selection and mutation are the only forces forming our brains, then why do we even have thoughts about anything that is not necessary for our survival? No creature, from microbe to monkey, sits around enjoying complex art or laying out the rules of logic. But suddenly (by evolutionary reckoning), we do. There is no other creature in nature that cares one iota what the true nature of things is. Why, under the sole influence of natural selection, would we have developed that need? If you follow out the logic of evolution, you have to conclude that the synapses we experience regarding survival and reproduction are reliable, while all others are just noise that should never have survived the natural-selection process.

Given all this, is it possible for anyone to really know how to accurately view our world? Is it possible to clearly and fully understand why we're here and how our world, our environment and the cosmos in which we live relate to us? In fact, can we really *know* anything?

All Knowledge Is Based on Faith in our Assumptions

Let's get back to objective knowledge. Science claims that if something is observable and testable, it can be known as true. We accept this, but is it really the case? Science is interested in finding empirical truth, which, of course, means truth that is verifiable based on experience or observation alone. *But the problem with gaining knowledge empirically is that all observations and conclusions are based on assumptions of the truth of things that are outside of science's ability to prove!* This makes scientific reasoning circular and its conclusions suspect. Can we really trust our experiences and observations?

In order to conduct an experiment and draw a factual conclusion from it, a scientist must rely on

- faith in the principles of logic,
- faith that his senses accurately convey reality to his brain,
- faith that the previously established axioms of science pertinent to the experiment are true in this and every future case (i.e., faith in what is known as the "uniformity of nature"),
- faith that he possesses the mental ability to accurately analyze his observations,
- faith in the adequacy of language to express his conclusions,
- faith that he is conscious and that his awareness of his surroundings is accurate (reference *The Matrix* movie trilogy),
- faith that he is not dreaming,[6]

---

[6] Descartes suggested that we cannot know, or prove, at any given time that we are not dreaming.

- faith that reason exists and that humans are capable of using it to make correct judgments,
- faith that his memory is capable of holding the facts (if that's what they are) that he has learned and that are needed to resolve the problem,
- faith that nature behaves reliably under all circumstances (another aspect of the uniformity of nature), and indeed,
- faith that truth itself exists.

These are all beliefs, or convictions, contained somewhere within the scientist that he trusts from experience but that cannot be proved scientifically. Each one requires, as stated in each example, a level of *faith*. Take the truth of any one of them away and science fails. Yet the "truths" that the scientist will confidently publish in a future science journal depend completely on them. David Marshall has put it this way:

> "…scientific evidence is based on faith—exactly the same kind of faith that informed Christians have in God. Science is always based on three kinds of reasonable, but fallible faith: trust in the mind, in the senses, and in other people. None of these can be proven—to use mind to prove mind is to argue in a circle. And the senses might be wrong. And there is no scientific test to prove our colleagues honest, reliable, competent—only social tests. Yet without reliance on all three, good science can't be done."[7]

---

[7] David Marshall, *The Truth Behind the New Atheism* (Eugene, OR: Harvest House, 2007).

So, before we can begin reasoning at all, we must rely on things that we have no way of proving. *The very knowledge that we exist* is an internal belief that cannot be proved scientifically. We internally assume, trust and believe that these "first principals"[8] are true, and they are the essential basis for what we claim to be empirically true. So we rely on *assumed truth* in order to arrive at *absolute truth*.[9]

This is not to imply that anyone believes these foundational principals are not true. As far as anyone knows, they certainly are. But the point is that *science*, based on naturalism, cannot verify them. In fact, naturalism, with its belief that all things arose from undirected accidents, logically conflicts with the idea that these principals are reliable. Why should uniform, reliable principals have arisen from chaos? But however we believe we arrived on this planet, we *must* assume these principals true or rationality falls to ruin. Encouraged by scientists, we tend to impute to science an omniscience that it falls woefully short of. C. S. Lewis (1898-1963) said that the business of science is to tell us what *normally* occurs.[10] That is, it describes how things behave each time they are tested. Beyond that, it can only speculate.

I submit that Christianity provides the only rational basis for trusting these beliefs.

Dr. Jason Lisle, astrophysicist and master of logic, points out that for any world view to be rational, it must provide a logical

---

[8] This term, from the science of logic, means things that we have to assume true in order to begin reasoning.

[9] "Absolute truth" is really a redundant expression. *Truth* is a synonym for how things really are, so by its nature, it's absolute. It would be best not to use modifiers to water down the word, such as *empirical, personal* or *relative*, because when you modify truth, you no longer have it. But it's commonly understood usage, so we do it anyway.

[10] C. S. Lewis, *Miracles* (New York: Harper Collins, 1947).

basis for believing that these underlying truths, or first principals, are reliable. A world view is unintelligible if these first principals are not supported by it. The Christian world view,[11] based on its understanding of God as given in the scriptures, supports the existence and reliability of these principals, which are the basis for organized and consistent reasoning, because an orderly and unchanging Creator established them in our reality. On naturalism, there is no reason to expect any truths that didn't arise from nature—certainly not orderliness, testability and reliability from a chaotic, undirected source. Both world views assume these first principals are true, but since naturalism has no justification for assuming them, it borrows from the Christian world view because it *must* assume them in order to begin reasoning at all. The idea that *"As long as the earth endures, seedtime and harvest, cold and heat, summer and winter, day and night will never cease"*[12] comes from scripture, the basis for the Christian world view. So a secular scientist contradicts himself when trusting in uniform and consistent behavior from a nature that arose from pre-molecular bedlam, while at the same time rejecting Christian beliefs. It doesn't take a professor of logic to see that it is illogical to base one's thinking on the truth of an opposing and completely contradictory viewpoint.[13]

Finally, and this is important, it is atypical for any scientist to approach any problem completely free of pre-decided opinions, or presuppositions, about that problem. Any researcher will claim that he follows the evidence wherever it leads, and he often believes this with all his heart, but it is almost never true. The search for knowledge is *virtually always* affected by our philosophical biases—the glasses through which we see the

---

[11] See Appendix A for a statement of the Christian world view.
[12] Genesis 8:22
[13] Concepts in this paragraph from: J. Lisle, *The Ultimate Proof of Creation* (Green Forest, AR: Master Books, 2009).

world. As twentieth-century French philosopher Henri Bergson (1859-1941) said, "The eye sees only what the mind is prepared to comprehend." It is *possible* to lay aside our biases and truly open our minds to possibilities we wouldn't have thought existed, but when it comes to matters that we feel strongly about, or that we have a prior commitment to, or that we have been thoroughly indoctrinated in, it is very rare for us to do so.

The search for knowledge is virtually always affected by our philosophical biases—the glasses through which we see the world.

As an example, many (even most) scientists assume before beginning an investigation that an explanation for any given problem can be found through the creative application of natural laws. This is what science is all about, and it's the approach that every scientist takes. Accordingly, since science is about nature, the idea that there could be an explanation from outside of nature is eliminated before beginning any investigation, and thereby, any findings are skewed. The reliability of this or any other kind of philosophical mindset can't be proved, but such biases are accepted as true as a conviction of the researcher before he or she even begins.

So knowing this adds another faith assumption that our scientist brings to each and every inquiry; namely,

- faith that his findings are not skewed by his own biases or those of others on whose results he depends.

This is something that few people even consider when reading or hearing about the various findings of science, but it is a fundamental question that should *always* be asked because it is virtually always a factor.

What Do We Really Know about Anything?

Science is spectacularly successful at discovering repeatable, demonstrable, physical truths in the present. That's why science produces wonderful achievements like space travel and computers. But scientists, just like you and me, are limited. No matter how much they may know about their field, when it comes to explaining the prehistoric past or understanding incredibly complex issues with many variables and imperfect data, they must speculate. In the case of prehistoric events, they weren't there to see them, and no amount of science in the present can definitively reveal how events unfolded to cause many of the things we see today. That's why popular explanations of these supposed past events are constantly changing. Scientists, because they are human, wear the glasses of their presuppositions and their limitations, just as everyone else does.

This problem of philosophical bias is, in fact, especially prevalent in the study of origins. One of many good examples of this is the way science has explained, over the years, the existence of our moon (and other moons). Many have tried to explain how it could be that a body such as the moon could be orbiting our planet at the distance and in the type of orbit that it does. The origin of a nearly perfect, circular orbit of one rocky body around another is hard to explain by natural forces over time. Also, given current theories about how such rocky bodies are formed in space, it's hard to come up with a plausible theory about how the material got there and formed a planetary body in the first place. Some have thought it was leftover matter from the formation of the earth that accreted into a moon rather than a planet.[14] Others postulated that the moon was formed as a small planet in the same way earth supposedly was, but elsewhere in the solar system, and that it was trapped gravitationally in orbit around our planet

---

[14] The accretion by gravitational attraction of solid objects in space to form planets and other bodies seems intuitively reasonable, but due to the laws of motion in a vacuum, the possibility is questioned by many.

as it passed by. But because of many physical difficulties with these theories, they were overturned in favor of the "Mars-sized impactor theory," which proposes that the earth was hit by a huge object. This object basically tore some of the material off of the earth, and after a long period of accretion, it ended up as our moon. Over time (the evolutionist's favorite ally), the earth healed of the wound. This is today's "theory du jour." But because this theory has insurmountable problems of its own, another will be along shortly to replace it (as soon as some imaginative scientist can think of one).

As I've said, such theories are not empirical science; they are attempts to theorize about unrepeatable events in the past by extrapolating backwards from what we see today and inserting theoretical events that *might have* caused the current situation. To espouse theories like these assertively is to step out of the proper realm of science and into the realm of dogma. If these theories were presented as ideas, or even "educated" conjecture, then we the public would know them for what they are. Instead, we are confidently led to believe that these are "discoveries" rather than speculations. Christians are admonished to test, or question, the spirit in which facts are presented to us to see if they comport with what God has told us about reality.[15] It would be nice if all students were taught to test what they are told against common sense and logic (in other words, what they already know intuitively about reality).

Because of the difficulties with the various proposed naturalist explanations, it's curious that I've never heard of an article published in a secular peer-reviewed journal saying that all conceivable naturalist theories are riddled with problems, so the moon probably has a supernatural origin (although at least one has come close). If scientists were truly unbiased truth-seekers,

---

[15] I John 4:1.

they would have to allow for such a possibility.

The moon, like so many other natural objects and circumstances, is critical to allowing life on earth. Why couldn't the moon have been placed there at the perfect distance and the perfect speed to create the required orbit to support life on our planet by an entity completely independent of natural limitations? Where secular science is concerned, it is because such an explanation is eliminated by the presupposition that all things have a natural explanation. And this presupposition exists primarily because an extra-natural explanation smacks much too plainly of the existence of a deity.

Because we are served this constant diet of naturalist thinking from nearly every information source available to us, we tend to think this way as well. We rarely bring to conscious thought the idea that the essential beliefs upon which we place our faith before we can even begin to examine and understand our reality may not be based on science or logic. Indeed, confidence in logic is one of these beliefs, so it would be a logical fallacy (circular reasoning) to say we believe them because they are logical! So where do they come from and on what are they based?

We All Have Faith in a Non-Physical Reality

It's worth reiterating that the above list of unprovable assumptions that a scientist needs in order to conduct an experiment all begin with the word *faith*. So since we always start our observation and reasoning with faith in assumptions, can we really, in an absolutely certain sense, say we *know* anything to be true? Because of these unproven beliefs that we hold as true, it could be said that ***all knowledge is based on faith*** because all knowledge *begins* with faith—faith that some essential and foundational things, things that we can't prove, are nevertheless true. Even facts that we consider conclusive are based on these underlying internal assumptions. These assumptions are examples of knowledge and belief present in our minds that do not come from the physical world and cannot be proved by scientific inquiry. So they are a result of *faith in a non-physical reality existing in all of us*, whether we admit it or not. We can believe ourselves fact-driven empiricists all we want, but the truth is that we all have a faith-based reality. So if a belief system based on faith is religion, we are all religious. But the point to remember is that God-based faith is rational because it provides the preconditions of rationality, while atheism-based faith is irrational based on its associated world view and because such faith is "borrowed" from its opposing world view.

> *If a belief system based on faith is religion, we are all religious.*

If you want to be technical, in the final analysis we really can't *prove* anything at all in the empirical sense because all of our methods of proof are based on our limited ability to test the physical world and sense the basic realities that may or may not underlie it. So we must base our methods on *assumed* truth. Although few people reason it out to this degree, every human being senses this, and often *it is the underlying basis for the bewilderment and lack of direction that characterize people's lives and for the vast differences in belief systems, values and judgment that we see among our human cohorts*. When a world view provides no solid basis for assuming underlying truth, nothing can be trusted as unshakably believable, and this inspires a deep insecurity in us. Why should one even try to understand the reason for and meaning of his existence if any answer he comes up with can be challenged by the holder of another belief system, or when the so-called "facts" of history, philosophy and science are modified regularly with every new wind of doctrine by those who claim they know? So, most people just remain befuddled. Any attempt at finding truth results in confusion, and we stop trying. In the deepest reaches of our minds, we are not sure we have a clue how things really are.

The Human Need for Meaning

If, on the other hand, all of these first principals, or foundational truths, were empirically provable, we might have a much more unified view of reality across our planet. And if we did, we would realize wonderful benefits (like peace and unity of purpose) that are missing because our understanding is confused and imperfect. We are all wearing different world-viewing glasses.

Still, although we understand that our grip on reality is weak, there is an internal need born into us that requires us to have *some* anchoring belief system, some meaning for our lives. This is why everyone espouses such a belief system, however unintelligible some of them may be. The book *Complete Idiot's Guide to World Religions* opens with this description of its first chapter:

> "Why Learn About Other Faiths? Discover how you can use the information in this book to… participate in the human family's ongoing search for meaning."[16]

This is a recurring theme throughout the philosophical writings of mankind, whether religious or secular. Apparently, even "complete idiots" want to participate in this search for meaning. Statements like this one, found everywhere, imply two underlying beliefs: that *life has, or should have, meaning,* and that it is

---

[16] B. Toropov and Fr. L. Buckles, *Complete Idiot's Guide to World Religions*, 3rd ed. (New York: Alpha Books, 2004).

important to discover what it is. Even those philosophers who have declared that life has no meaning at all have spent near lifetimes searching for that very thing. It is a matter of the highest importance to every human.

How, then, can we make sense of our existence and why do we so clearly need to? The answers begin with accepting the idea that there is an objective reality and a truth that exists independent of the natural or material world. If human inquiry into the natural world falls short of explaining reality, then maybe such explanations come from outside that world. The word *supernatural*, which is feared and shied away from by many, merely means *existing outside of the natural*. If a thing is not made of matter (or its counterpart, energy) and subject to natural laws, then it is supernatural. These truths that we've been discussing, on which we base our faith, are supernatural because they exist inside our psyches. They cannot be touched, smelled, heard, tasted or seen. They do not obey natural laws, and they resist quantifying. They are not of the natural world, so they are supernatural.

Further, we do not require proof that these things exist. They are characterized by the fact that we cannot conceive of their opposite, or that if we imagine they are untrue, the structure of our reality begins to crumble. The point cannot be overemphasized—these things exist outside of the physical world, and because of that they are, by definition, supernatural. So before reaching very deeply into our discussion here, we have already discovered things that exist outside of the tangible world.

Right and Wrong, Good and Bad

The same principle applies to moral truth. A great number of moral truths exist within us that cannot be dealt with by the scientific method. As an example, it is known within us that abusing children for fun and profit is wrong. To us, it is intrinsically wrong, and the fact that it is wrong need not be proved in order for a healthy mind to know it. Certainly the most committed atheist/materialist would agree with this (though in reality, it is inconsistent with their world view[17]). Within ourselves and without the benefit of physical proof, we know that there are things that are wrong. It's not that we don't do these things because we've found them to be less than useful in our culture—it's that we see them as objectively wrong. It's not that psychologically healthy people avoid them because they're illegal and we might pay a price for doing them, it's because their "wrongness" is an internal prejudice born in us. Conversely, we know without proof that some things are right

> *We…know instinctively that there should be some moral significance to our lives, even if we don't know what it is.*

and/or good. We crave relationships with other humans, enjoy art, music and beauty and seek justice and truth (as we're doing here). We don't have to prove that truth, beauty and relationships are good, and we don't see them that way because we are following majority opinion. We just know it. There will be more on this in the next chapter.

We also know instinctively that there should be some moral significance to our lives, even if we don't know what it is. We know without proof that there is, or at least should be, a reason why we exist, despite a lifetime of hearing naturalist claims that we are a mere biological accident. The understanding of these things exists

---

[17] That is, if children are just examples of rearranged molecules from some "warm little pond" like all other living things, why should they enjoy status higher than, say, an ant, or a snake?

in us at birth. They are present in every healthy human from the beginning of his existence.

But man is a stubborn creature. Christians believe that man's natural tendency is to believe himself equal with (or perhaps superior to) God. Hardly any human would say it out loud; we prefer to say we don't believe in Him, which of course is saying the same thing because not believing in any god makes us "god" of our own lives. So, the last thing we want to do is to confront the reality of elements of our being which we know full well do not arise from the physical world. We may acknowledge these elements, but this is where many people stop thinking, because to continue a logical train of thought from this fact is to admit that a supernatural world does exist, and that implies the possibility of a supernatural source of the natural world because we realize that nature cannot create itself.[18] If we were to allow ourselves to reason this far, we would be hard pressed to deny the reality of a Creator, thereby implying that there may exist an entity which should properly have authority over us. Mankind's arrogance will not allow this.

Can Anything Be Known Unquestionably?

So, back to the point of this chapter: what do we really know? Not much, if we lean on our own reason, understanding that we believe so many things that we can't prove. Perhaps we can look to Plato for help. He defined knowledge as "justified true belief." If we go by that, believing on reasoned faith in an orderly, consistent, trustworthy Law Giver that our internal assumptions about reality are valid, and realizing that they cannot have arisen from nature, we can know quite a bit. If we

---

[18] I know of no naturalist who has ever postulated a true *source* for the natural world. But since an infinite regression of causes is illogical, such a source must exist. The Big Bang Theory, among its many problems, makes no attempt to explain the cause of the original "singularity" that theoretically exploded.

start from that world view, foundational truths on which we depend are "justified" by our beliefs. But if no such Law Giver exists, there exists no justification except experience for trusting the things we take for granted. Based on a world view that all reality arose from indiscriminate accidents, faith that our experiences will continue in the future as they have in the past is not justified. The fact that they will continue as such is a true belief, but on a materialist world view, it is not a "justified" belief, so according to Plato, it is not knowledge. In a way, for the atheist, it is true, ironically, by accident.[19]

But because there *is* an omnipotent Law Giver, we can know and be confident, based on our justified true belief, that many things have been measured and studied by man to the degree that they can reasonably be trusted as fact. But we must understand that all facts rest on faith-based axioms and *some* things that we consider facts are actually interpretations of evidence based on philosophical biases.

Nonetheless, there is a way that we can know that our world, or our life, or reality, has dimensions that are more than physical. We can know that we can't know everything. We can know that we need faith in a being more powerful than ourselves in order to arrive at ultimate truth. We can know that this truth is objective; that it is true everywhere, at all times, and under all circumstances and that it cannot be modified by the opinion of men. We can know that we are not really the masters of our own fate. We can understand that our reasoning is limited and weak, and that we are not the best choice for ruler of our lives. And we can know that some things are, without doubt or ambiguity, either good or evil. Hopefully, as you read on you will see what I mean.

---

[19] Thanks again to Dr. Jason Lisle and his book, *The Ultimate Proof of Creation*, cited earlier, for helping me more clearly explain justified true belief.

Chapter Two

Who Are We and Why Are We Here?

"You enter the brain through the eye, march up the optic nerve, round and round the cortex, looking behind every neuron, and then, before you know it you emerge into daylight on the spike of a motor nerve impulse, scratching your head and wondering where the self is."
—*Daniel Clement Dennett*

Having established the existence of certain inborn, supernatural truths and needs within us, we can begin to answer the question, "Why do we so intensely need to make sense of our existence?" The answer is simple: we feel that need because we know instinctively and supernaturally that there is purpose behind nature and behind our personal existence.

No reasonably healthy human fails to understand instinctively the relationship between cause and effect. This understanding is programmed into even the most simple among us. We certainly understand that many things can be caused by accidental random forces, but that same reasoning power gives us an understanding that when a thing has a purpose, it was designed and built for that purpose by an intelligence greater than its own. This incredibly simple truth is often disregarded in naturalist philosophy whenever it points toward a supernatural cause.

When a thing has been intelligently caused, we know that there is always a reason. Conversely, when something exists for a reason, we know that it was intelligently caused. Even when we do something as simple as choosing to kick a stone as we walk and talk, we do it for a reason. We might say we had no reason, but the truth is we did it because we had an impulse to see the stone fly or because we needed a momentary distraction from our thoughts or from the conversation. The movement of the rock, because it was caused by intelligence, had a reason arising from that intelligence, simple though the reason might have been.

Specified Complexity

Given this fact, consider the human being. At the very least, we humans are incredibly complex[1] machines able to accomplish myriad physical tasks, never mind reasoning, morality, and so forth. On the most basic biological level, we human machines are obviously built for the *purpose* of sustaining and reproducing ourselves. For this purpose, we have various mobility mechanisms, a clever brain and bodily systems to sustain us. We obviously have at least basic purposes as complex organisms. So the natural understanding within us (i.e., common sense) tells us that we must be intelligently designed for at least these simple purposes.

Complexity with purpose arises only from purposeful design.

---

[1] "Incredibly complex" is a massive understatement. There is nothing in the physical world that remotely approaches the complexity of the human being.

Complexity with purpose (sometimes called "specified complexity") arises only from purposeful design. No human being has ever observed or recorded anything that contradicts this axiom.

But we humans have a great many more abilities than just to eek out survival and find a mate. Alone among species, we can communicate with each other in complex language, reason with each other, investigate our environment in more detail by countless multiples than any of our fellow species, have close relationships based on mutual self-denial and genuine concern for each other's well-being, understand and put to use complicated information systems, imagine a better world and many other non-physical abilities far above those of any other type of creature. And we alone have it in our nature to want to know why we are different in this way. These abilities are completely inexplicable under any materialist world view.

The Real "You"

I have said that we know within ourselves that we are dichotomous beings. We realize there is more to us than that which can be sensed in a physical way. We know we are part natural and part supernatural, both physical and spiritual. But *how* do we know this? How does that knowledge arrive in us as humans?

Christianity posits that the *self* that the atheist philosopher Daniel Dennett, in the opening quote of this chapter, can't seem to find is a kind of *"you"* that is not available to the physical world. Think about it. You are the only person in the world that can know *you* on a completely intimate level. The way you feel about things, the outlook you have, your true motivations, the effect of experiences on you, these are things that you can only partially explain to another person. We all understand that no one knows us on the level we know ourselves. One of the challenges of authoring a book like this one is that the author will inevitably fail to fully communicate at least some of his feelings, thoughts, or impressions in the way he hopes to for any particular reader. And one reader will experience any book a little differently than another. So on a moment-by-moment basis, we all experience a *self* awareness that is unique to us, separate from others and completely non-physical. There is something within us that we have no doubt exists, but we are aware of it in ways that have nothing to do with sight, touch, taste, hearing or smell. These five senses are designed for experiencing the physical world, but they are useless for perceiving our unique spiritual self.

This is the *"you"* that will live forever. It is you on the true level of *being*. While philosophy calls this the self, God (as translated by English-speaking humans) calls it the *soul*.

Suppose you are an accountant for a living. While compiling a tax return, you can direct your brain to enter calculations into the computer, and your brain can delegate your fingers to the task. But it would be silly to say that your fingers and your brain are doing the accounting. They have no ability to *do* accounting. They have only the biological and physical mechanisms required for *you* to do it. A brain and fingers are useless unless *something* decides to make the entries and directs these mechanisms to carry out its decision. Who or what is that *something*? A collection of inanimate atoms and molecules? Or is it something beyond atoms and molecules; something non-physical? At a minimum, this *something* would include reason, will, conscience (the compulsion to do the accounting properly) and motivation (to receive some sort of reward for the effort.) These are not the expressions of a physical body, they are the expressions of the real *you*.

The Christian world view presupposes that awareness of this supernatural "us" was placed in our minds by a supernatural source. We know that this source must exist because of our internal axiom of causation that I discussed above. If we can rely on logic at all, then we have to believe that a supernatural reality cannot logically arise from a natural one, so the source of the part of our being which is not natural would have to be supernatural. We have learned from experience, and from science—real, observational science—that nature is bounded, and it cannot create or interact with something outside itself (nor can it create itself). This is why we can never fully know the "*self*" of another person. We interface with them only through our senses, which cannot reach their spiritual self.[2] Only God can reach us on that level. It is reserved for Him.

The Internal Moral Yardstick

So, it is this spiritual self within us that contains such things as our objective yardstick of right and wrong by which we measure all that we experience in the physical world. I discussed in chapter one that we know right and wrong and good and bad exist and that all of mankind has the same basic outline of what each of those are. This is different from the yardstick that is given to animals telling them what they should and should not do in their world. Their evaluation of right and wrong is based on their God-given instinct for survival and drive for reproduction within their established order, just as ours would be were evolution in charge of our development. Animals apply their "world view" in an instinctive response to stimuli, and their ability to choose whether or not to follow it is limited. There is in reality no moral good or bad included in their world view. What one animal might do to another is morally irrelevant

---

[2] Many of us do believe that our souls can communicate with each other on a spiritual level in certain circumstances, but that's a proposition to be argued another day.

because they are simply responding to bodily cues built into them. Our instinctive understanding of moral values and duties, on the other hand, goes far beyond mere responses to our physical environment and encompasses all that we will experience in our lives, both the physical and the spiritual experiences, and we are free to ignore it if we choose.

This "yardstick," often so-called because it is a measure against which we compare our behavior and choices, is an internal understanding that by logical inference must have come from an entity outside ourselves who establishes this *rightness* and *wrongness* standard and who has placed this knowledge within us. This concept is formally known as *The Moral Argument* (for the existence of God) in modern theological apologetics. It goes like this: if our standard

> *Our standard for moral values and duties... must have come from some sort of law giver who imprinted it in human consciousness.*

for moral values and duties is indeed *objective*, that is, it exists independently of what any individual might think of it, then it cannot have originated with any individual or group of individuals. It must have come from some sort of law giver who imprinted it in human consciousness. If it originated in any way with humans, then it would be based on the ideas, needs, and current popular thinking of a given society and would *not* transcend human thinking or be the same no matter the time, place or situation. What we find, though, is that core values and moral duties are the same from culture to culture over our entire recorded history.

Now in thinking this idea through, a lot of people get lost in details. Some will say, *that's not true. The ancient Greeks (Romans, etc.) had very different core values and duties from those of modern cultures. Many under-developed societies have brutal and harsh practices that they value as good. And there are many other examples of this.* We'll talk more in a few pages about the fact that man is capable of denying his conscience and convincing himself that what he knows to be true is in fact not true at all. If one looks at all of recorded history as a continuum, however, one has to agree that societies have generally had similar beliefs about the core elements of right and wrong. This is true regardless of the many and varied aberrations that decadent or underdeveloped societies have indulged in from time to time. While the men of the Roman elite convinced themselves for a time that fondling young boys or forcing gladiators to kill each other for their entertainment was acceptable, the rest of the world was living as best they could by the values impressed upon their psyches. Even when various people groups throughout history were able to convince themselves that certain other groups were far less valuable than themselves and felt little compunction in murdering or enslaving them on a whim, they still refrained from murdering or enslaving the members of what they considered their own privileged group. Why? Because murder and slavery were as wrong to them as they are to us. For complicated reasons imposed on them by their culture, they suppressed the knowledge within them that all human life is equally valuable. If they had not been influenced to suppress it, their natural understanding of life's intrinsic value would have prevented them from acting in the way that they did. No matter the specific behavior of a given person, group or society in any given time period, recognizable, objective values and morals are still present among them, and significantly, these aberrations always pass with time, allowing society to return to these eternal, objective values.

This should not be mistaken for a claim that all humans are basically good. We'll discuss in later chapters why exactly the opposite is true. But throughout history, even while men or societies who have steeled their consciences against the Giver of moral law have done *"what was right in their own eyes,"*[3] the core values and morals of humankind have endured, and these societies have eventually reaped their just reward and passed away, allowing this repressed objective morality to rise to the surface and again dominate the human conscience. No matter the temporary aberration, whether it's Communism, Nazi-ism, Hellenistic cultures, hippie-ism and other sub-cultures, primitive cultures, or of particular consequence to us, the decadent cultures of today, human core morality exists and endures.

Consider what the only reasonable expectation about morals would be if naturalism were true. The only physical or natural basis for judging a thing good or bad would be whether or not it advanced the survival of ourselves and possibly our immediate gene pool or whether or not it made us feel physically good along the way. But we are born with numerous intrinsic presuppositions about moral goodness and badness that have nothing to do with our physical needs or instincts.

> *If a perfect, eternal Being does not exist, then there exists no source of objective values...*

It is upon them that we base our understanding of right and wrong, good and bad. Based on naturalism, we should have developed a whole different basis for making value judgments—one similar to that of the rest of nature. Like the other creatures of the world, what we may or may not do to each other should be morally irrelevant. What serves to perpetuate us and our genetic material we should do, what interferes we should avoid.

But again, in the species *Homo sapiens* alone we find a much different system of setting value on different elements of life. Where did this come from if only "survival of the fittest" drove

---

[3] Wording from Judges 21:25, KJV.

our species to where it is today? There are those, like Dennett, who argue that our value systems really do arise from a kind of "evolutionary psychology," that our values do in fact stem from the environmental pressures of our ancestors. But the reasoning is a stretch and not widely accepted even among secular psychologists. It is based on the imagination of men with a prior commitment to materialism. To imagine that we developed conscience, altruism, moral values and so forth because our ancestors found that such tactics "worked" in their battle to survive is to deny the rest of the principles of natural selection. Such arguments usually don't address where the rest of the strictly human pursuits came from, such as love of art, music and beauty, desire for deeply committed personal relationships, and the love of knowledge and wisdom. And finally, such attempts at explaining the evolution of higher values almost never offer a story about why such development occurred only in us among all the species of the earth.

The Christian understanding of this innate ability to discern right from wrong comes not only from logic, but directly from the scriptures which drive our world view. They say this:

> *"Indeed, when [people] who do not have [God's] law, do by nature things required by the law, they are a law for themselves...since they show that <u>the requirements of the law are written on their hearts</u>, their consciences also bearing witness, and their thoughts now accusing, now...defending them."* [4]

Here again, the Christian world view provides the requisite precondition for the idea of objective morality in the cultures of our world to be intelligible. Atheist world views based on

---

[4] Romans 2:14 & 15.

materialism do not. There is no reason based on atheism to believe that objective morals exist. The atheist or secularist may fight the idea all she likes and may find some comfort in the plentiful writings of philosophers of like mind, but in her heart of hearts, her soul if you will, she has inscribed the divine yardstick of good and bad, right and wrong. No getting around it; if a perfect, eternal Being does not exist, then there exists no source of objective values, and all are subjective (established by each individual) and relative (to the given situation). The naturalist should feel justified in deciding for herself whether and in what circumstance murder, rape, theft, dishonesty, selfishness and hate are wrong, and when they are justified. But most of these things are seen as objectively wrong in all of the world's societies. The only explanation is that it has nothing to do with societies. Its source, as explained in the Bible reference above, transcends societies and human thinking. It is written on the human heart by the Creator God.

The Basic Attributes of God

In addition to just knowing that this law giver exists, we are also born with the understanding that this is a *personal* entity in the sense that it must possess a personality, because it must have *chosen* to place this understanding within us. It cannot be merely an unknowable spiritual force, because a mere spiritual force could not create. It takes a will to be a creator. A will is an element of personality.

So, let's recap some of the basic characteristics of the Christian God that we've discovered so far: He is a moral, self-aware, personal entity existing outside of nature, of which He is the source. He is capable of interacting with nature and as the Creator of its laws; He is not bound by them. Such an entity, with at least these basic characteristics, *must* exist because of the presence in us of knowledge and understanding unexplainable by nature itself and because of the existence of many realities that could not have arisen from nature. Moreover, *this entity must possess knowledge and capability vastly superior to our own,* because it is able to place this knowledge within our being and establish these transcendent realities.

Every life begins with an awareness of this God. But many, due to myriad different circumstances, never search out and study Him. Without making the effort to study Him, how much would every person know about this Being?

Christians believe that God (the Being in question) has answered this question for us. According to the revealed word of the Creator, we are intrinsically aware of the essential parts of His nature:

> *"...what may be known about God is plain to [mankind], because God has made it plain to them. For since the creation of the world God's invisible qualities— his eternal power and divine nature—have been clearly seen, being understood from what has been made, so that men are without excuse."*[5]

In other words, we know *enough*. This passage tells us that everything we see in the natural world—its complexity, its beauty, and its order—is a confirmation to our minds that there must be something outside of nature that has caused all that we see. Without scientific or academic input from any source, we know that nature is derived from a creator outside itself. This has been

Universal, invariant laws are a reflection of the Creator's unchanging essence.

---

[5] Romans 1:19 & 20.

known by every mentally healthy person since time began, and not just known, but "clearly seen." This verse goes on to say that humankind not only knows there is a God but understands plainly a great deal of what He is like!

Moreover, we don't have to be taught to understand that the *laws* of both reason and nature are supernatural (not made of matter and existing outside of the material world). These laws in a sense rule the natural world, operating as their Creator has commanded them to, from outside it. Unless God intervenes, they apply consistently everywhere and at all times (as far as we know). They are, in fact, the basis for the godless theories man has constructed to posit that nature is all there is. Yet there is no rational basis for contending that these laws arose *from* nature, because they are not *of* nature. So, secular humankind bases its materialist theories on a supernatural reality: the laws of nature. This, as I've labored to point out, is a self-contradictory methodology. If these laws rule nature, they could not have arisen from it. The position that the laws of nature *created* nature, or that nature created its own laws, is absurd and should be easily rejected by any rational mind.

The Christian would submit that universal, invariant laws are a reflection of the Creator's unchanging essence. The rules of reason we employ are orderly, absolute and immaterial because their source, our God, is consistent, sovereign and spiritual. It is another way in which we know of His existence and His character.

For Your Information

One of the most powerful confirmations that a supernatural world exists, for me, is the existence of information systems. If you think about it, the natural world is made up of molecules and atoms and quarks and God knows (literally) what all else, but something like an information system cannot possibly arise from these elements of matter. It cannot be physically caused, randomly or otherwise. It can certainly be present in matter (for instance, in the form of ink on paper, as it is here), but wherever we find it expressed in matter, we know that it was always placed there, ultimately, by a causal source who intended for it to be there.

In order to have information, we have to have some sort of system of meaningful symbols and a coded way of arranging them in order for a sender to communicate an idea, or a request, or whatever. Whether the medium is spoken language, written word, patterned radio waves, art, music, facial expressions or any other communication system imaginable, an intelligent source has to have initiated the transfer of the information. If there is a way that such a system can arise from undirected atoms and molecules, I would like to hear about it. No one has ever even claimed, I don't think, that a material entity can create a non-material one. Indeed, materialism claims that there are no non-material entities.

Yet in our bodies, we have a massive, though incredibly compact, information nano-system far more sophisticated than any mankind has ever developed or discovered. It is expressed in or carried upon the incredible DNA molecule, but the molecule itself is not the information. The matter does not give meaning to the symbols contained in it. If the symbols contained in the DNA—combinations of just four nucleotide molecules—take on meaning, it is because of the code (meaningful method of arranging the symbols) that has been imposed upon them by a sender. This is one of the many God-given, internal understandings that we have as humans: information is sent by an intelligent source. It doesn't just accidentally arise from inanimate matter. So it follows that this sender must have encoded the information in the molecules and constructed the biological machines that would respond to (decode) the information and carry out its instructions.

There is no explanation for a system of symbology, encoding and decoding existing in a purely material world. I don't think any scientist would deny this. Yet in Mountain View, California, the ardent secularists of the S.E.T.I. (Search for Extra-Terrestrial Intelligence) project, who believe everything arises from randomness, spend millions of taxpayers' dollars looking for signs of intelligent life by listening to our universe for patterns in the random radio signals found in space. Why? Because they know that only intelligence can give rise to communication patterns. If they find a patterned signal, they know that it would have to have been sent by an intelligence. So the whole basis of their experiment mocks their world view: Life contains examples of almost indescribably complex information and communication systems which, according to their world view, occurred randomly (no intelligence was behind them). At the same time, they look for intelligence by searching for information transmitted from space, because they know such information can only arise from intelligence. Someone else will have to explain that reasoning, because I can't.

> *Many...non-physical realities exist in our world. Atheism has the hopeless task of convincing us that these can somehow arise accidentally from nature.*

Self awareness, objective morality, knowledge and awareness of God, laws of logic and nature, information systems, will, purpose, curiosity, first causes, mathematics, and many other non-physical realities exist in our world. Atheism has the hopeless task of convincing us that somehow these can arise accidentally from nature.

Mankind's Persistent Arrogance

We have said that all humans know these truths and hold them strongly because they are a part of us from the beginning of our existence. But men are tenacious in their desire to justify ruling themselves, and because God has made the human mind powerful enough, with dogged persistence over time, to reason away some of this intrinsic knowledge, men attempt to do exactly that. This is a mortal danger faced by the soul (or the self) of every person: the possibility of erasing, through the unrelenting insistence of the arrogant human mind, some of the all-important knowledge placed in us by the Creator. We observe this nearly everywhere we look in our world's cultures, but it is also revealed to us through God's word:

> *"Men...<u>suppress the truth</u> by their wickedness... For although they knew God, they neither glorified him as God, nor gave thanks to Him; but their thinking became futile and their foolish hearts were darkened."* [6]

So although all men have a basic outline of God implanted in their psyche at birth, care must be taken to prevent the misuse of their reason, which may convince them that their inborn knowledge is mistaken. Note that once a man denies the truth within him, he loses his ability to reason effectively (his thinking becomes futile) about this matter of God. As the King James Version of the Bible translates it, "they became vain in their imaginations." It is man's vanity and arrogance that cause him to dismiss God and invent his own version of reality, and when he does this, his vanity is multiplied until his desire to rule over himself causes him to imagine anything necessary, no matter how ludicrous, in order to convince himself that he needn't

---

[6] Romans 1:18, 21.

worry about the idea of a God. This is the sad reality of our secular culture today.

But it needn't be so. If a person will seek this inborn knowledge of basic truths of his surroundings, basic moral truths and basic outline of the source of these truths born in all humans, his eyes will be re-opened to a reasoned belief in the supernatural world and a Creator. God has promised that if a person truly seeks, he will certainly find this truth.[7] The existence of a supernatural reality can't be proved, but Christians believe that it exists because we know that these examples of it exist within us. To deny it is to deny a part of ourselves, in the same way as if we were to deny the internal organs of our body that we can't see but we know are a part of us. Such a denial can certainly be made, and it *is* made daily by huge numbers across our planet, but it is done as a deliberate choice of the self-important human mind, and this does not change the reality of its existence. In a sense, this is what the whole question of religion versus naturalism is all about: the choice of accepting what we start out knowing to be true or replacing it with what we in our self-alleged wisdom decide is true. C. S. Lewis put it like this: "There are only two kinds of people: Those who say to God, 'Thy will be done' or those to whom God in the end says, 'All right then, have it your way.'"[8]

The Blessing, and Curse, of Curiosity

This basic inborn knowledge of the reality of a Creator is not enough, in itself, to satisfy us. This is one reason why people get off track in seeking more information about reality. Just knowing that a supernatural world exists and having a basic understanding of the power and nature of the Creator is not

---

[7] Matthew 7:7, 8.
[8] C. Lewis, *The Screwtape Letters* (New York: Harper Collins, 1942).

enough for our curious minds. For the same reason that we take our basic understanding of our physical environment and are driven to build on that by scientific analysis, we have the same kind of need to know more about this basic supernatural information that is born in us. God has placed within us enough knowledge about both the natural and the supernatural worlds to create within us a thirst to know more. Curiosity is itself another inborn, supernatural need that causes us to seek higher levels of truth. In seeking this truth, whether about physical or spiritual reality, we come closer to knowing the Author of all truth. In this process, whether in a scientific, academic or religious setting, we are seeking God, and we do this because of the need He has placed within us. It's important to understand that everyone experiences this process to some degree. Even the person who eventually pronounces himself an atheist has investigated his world in search of truth. Since God is the very personification of truth, this atheist has been seeking God. He's just lost the trail of Him somehow along the way.

In seeking...truth...we come closer to knowing the Author of all truth.

The trouble with trying to expand on our intrinsic understanding of God is that, like history, it can't be subjected to a laboratory analysis. We sometimes try, and this effort is often a large part of the reason that some, in the end, pronounce Him dead. In order to force spiritual searching into the mold of physical searching, we have to eliminate the non-physical (i.e., spiritual) elements of it! We try to apply the same methodology that we use in physical science to our search for spiritual truth. This can't be done, yet trying to do it is the basis for modern secular academic disciplines aimed at explaining life. Even Daniel Dennett appears, according to the opening quote of this chapter, to realize (though he goes on to deny it) that the essence of the *self*—who we are and what that means—cannot be found by studying the physical nature of personhood. There is more to us than that. We know that this is true no matter how many times or how dogmatically we've been told that we were formed by natural accidents, or how fervently Dennett and his ilk preach it. We have an impossibly high level of complexity that is ordered, and directed, and purposeful. And we exist beyond the physical. Christians believe that we are made in God's image, with many of His attributes,[9] such as emotion, reason, altruism, love, curiosity and a sense of right and wrong. No matter how much human imagination[10] is applied to materialistic thinking, these cannot be explained by nature. And we cannot discover the truth by postulating strictly physical hypotheses to explain them. Any such hypothesis runs into immediate trouble. This is why it is so hard for those like Dennett, who reject a spiritual reality, to explain the meaning of life.

The Purpose of Our Existence

C. S. Lewis suggested, "If I find in myself a desire which no experience in this world can satisfy, the most probable explanation is that I was made for another world."[11] The Christian world view sees man as created for the purpose of having a relationship with his Creator. We are essentially spiritual beings made for another world. We are a "soul," so that we can be loved by a spiritual God and learn to love Him back by practicing love in the way that His word teaches us to and realizing the benefits of it. We are here to enjoy and care for the

---

[9] But also lacking many, such as omniscience, omnipotence, omnipresence, perfect love, perfect wisdom and so forth.

[10] As will be pointed out in the next chapter, the imagination of man is not one of the legitimate sources of truth. It is very important to keep this in mind.

[11] C.S. Lewis, *Mere Christianity* (San Francisco: Harper, 2007)

things He has created for us, to learn and grow, to share what we have learned so that others can grow as well, and ultimately, to decide who will rule our lives. God knows that these are the things that will satisfy and fulfill the true, inner *us*. We are free to do all, any or none of the things He has created us to do, because before time, He committed Himself to loving us enough to make us free. There is a saying most have heard that goes something like this: *if you love something, set it free. If it comes back to you, then it is truly yours. If it doesn't, it never was.* This saying has become passé in our culture, but it is wisdom that reflects the way God Himself loves us.

Who are we? To put it succinctly, we are eternal, though temporarily embodied, spiritual creatures created to provide a place into which God's love and joy can flow. We are beings into which His love can expand and express itself.

Why are we here? We are here to experience and enjoy God's love and His creation, to learn how to know the joy of loving Him back, to learn the benefits of trusting Him and worshipping Him, to know the fulfillment of sharing the knowledge of Him with others and to eventually put off our physical bodies and live in an intimate, loving relationship with Him forever.

Chapter Three

What Is Christianity Anyway?

"The Christian ideal has not been tried and found wanting; it has been found difficult and left untried."
—*G. K. Chesterton*

What then, is the essential nature of Christianity? How can it be defined? Which of the many Christian preachers, priests and prophets, all conflicting with one another, has it right? Should one listen to the doctrine of some TV evangelist, one of the mega-church pastors or the local parish priest? And why do Christianity's adherents seem to be as flawed and confused as the rest of humanity? Does this belief system turn *all* its devotees into phony office evangelists? Why in the world should one choose this religion over any other?

Religion versus Christianity

First, Christianity is not a religion in the sense that I will define it here. This will sound strange to some, but to understand Christianity as a religion is to bring to it the baggage of misunderstanding that man has laid upon the word "religion" over the centuries. Religion, properly defined, is the belief system in which we place our faith and trust. But people don't define it properly. The words *religion* and *faith* often get used interchangeably, but they are different things. Anything can be a religion to a given person. Our religion is the thing on which we rely for our security —the thing in which we, wisely or unwisely, place our highest faith and trust. Many people's religion is their career. Others worship love as the thing on which they can ultimately rely. Some people make a religion out of being good, or being a person of high character, while a lot of people today are making science their ultimate authority. And sadly, we know that over the centuries, many worldwide have integrated their ancient rivalries, prejudices, resentments and political views into an existing faith-based belief system as a vehicle for justifying vengeful atrocities against their enemies, whether real or imagined, thereby placing their faith not in the belief system, but in vengeance and domination of others. It might be fair to call these and other expressions of faith religion, but they are not what I am describing here.

One's religion can also be the *form* designated by a chosen religious organization for expressing one's faith. In this case, a person places faith in the formal *practice* of his beliefs, or the ritual observance of them rather than in the tenets of the faith itself. Here, religion is *how* a person worships, or what she believes is the proper way to experience and express her beliefs. It is trusting in going to church, singing hymns, praying ritual prayers, repeating liturgies and so forth—a kind of religion of obedience.

Finally, religion can refer to an institutionalized political force—the organization that adherents to a belief system have put in place. Like any organization, an organized "religion" functions like an individual in society. It interacts with a culture, has relationships with it and with individuals, and gains and loses positional power within the culture. As such, it is capable of all the good and all of the evil any individual can achieve.

Christianity, though, if properly understood, is very different from these definitions of religion. In reality, this is true of any faith-based belief system. A belief system is a set of presuppositions that are accepted as true. The acceptance of these biases is in turn based, one hopes, on a logical and reasonable faith in their source. Christianity is a belief system based on faith in a personal deity. It is a systematic approach to understanding what is true about our existence on this planet, with an emphasis on what is true about our relationship to God. If religion were always defined strictly in this way, without expanding it to include all of the other things listed above (and more), then I would be happy with defining Christianity as a religion. In its essential nature, though, Christianity has nothing to do with any church, religious institution or particular individual (other than Jesus Christ). Although groups of believers and the organization of those groups (including leadership and so forth) are sanctioned in scripture, neither the believers themselves nor the organizations formed by those believers defines the belief system. In evaluating any belief system, it is important to separate its tenets from the actions of its adherents.

> *Christianity…is a systematic approach to understanding what is true about our existence on this planet…*

The Importance of Transcendent Truth

Christianity is based on unchangeable, transcendent truth. I have spent so much time on the nature of truth because Christianity ultimately depends on the ability to be completely confident in and dependent upon a foundational, immutable truth about how things really are. Pastor and author John MacArthur puts it clearly when he writes, "Truth—including historical facts, assurance, and objective, distinct, knowable, authoritative propositions that demand to be embraced as true—is an essential concept in authentic Christianity. All the other aspects of religious experience flow from the truth we believe and simply give expression to it. Take away the ground of truth, and all you have is fluctuating religious sentiment."[1] This system of viewing the world relies upon the conviction that there are certain objective truths that are unshakeable by man's ever-changing beliefs. Because they *are* true, they will always *be* true. One can rely on them in any culture and in any era because they are dependent on nothing.

Furthermore, there are only two places in which truth—beyond the truth that is preexistent in our conscience at birth—can be discovered by man. These places are *Divine Revelation*[2] and *Human Reason.* These two work together, the latter relying on the former, to inform us accurately of our world. The origin of both is the God of the universe. Divine revelation is information that has been given to man by the all-knowing Creator through what we today call scripture. The Christian presupposes this information to be true by a faith that arises from reason. Reason

> *There are certain objective truths that are unshakeable by man's ever-changing beliefs.*

---

[1] J. MacArthur, *The Truth War, Fighting for Certainty in an Age of Deception* (Nashville: Thomas Nelson, 2007).

[2] Divine revelation here refers to both *special revelation* and *general revelation*, which are often-used theological terms. Special revelation refers to the Bible, while general revelation refers to the testimony of nature itself, as described in the Bible (Rom. 1:19, 20). General revelation is subordinate to special revelation because special revelation is the direct declaration of the Creator, while general revelation is revealed indirectly through His works and must be interpreted by fallible mankind.

is the way in which we gain confidence that certain things are true because they comport with what is known through revelation, through our experience and inquiry, and through our powers of logic, which are also given to us by our Creator. Human reason is subordinate to revelation because revelation proceeds from an Entity that has perfect knowledge of things beyond the scope of our experience and that possesses perfect reasoning ability, while human reasoning is highly fallible. Having accepted this revealed truth by reasoned faith, we learn not to pervert our powers of reason by imagining that life can be explained in any way contrary to it. The use of reason is what leads us to accept revelation on faith. Revelation is what gives us a solid foundation of truth from which to reason. This intricate dance of cooperation between reason and revelation is what brings us to the point of understanding our reality and prepares us for a fulfilling relationship with our Creator.

Reason, of course, also leads us to much truth that God has not chosen to reveal to us through His word. We use our reason to discover truths about our world, especially the physical world that God has left for us to find for ourselves. But to imagine that fallible human reason is powerful enough to overturn revealed truth is to imagine that the created ones are somehow able to learn higher truths about their environment than the One who created them. Protestant reformer Martin Luther (1483-1546) condemned this as the "magisterial" use of reason. He said that the proper use of reason, the "ministerial" use, was to *understand* the revealed truth, rather than to pass judgment on it.

If Christianity is correctly understood, these two, revelation and reason, work together in their proper roles, supported by each other and leading to faith, in accordance with this system of belief. This faith, then, which arises from revealed and rationally derived truth, leads to ever deeper understanding of the complex and difficult aspects of our reality and our relationship with God.

Please note specifically that I have not mentioned personal experience as a valid source of truth. It is very important for seekers of truth to understand that personal experience does not establish truth, at least for others. This is why it is so ineffective for Christians, or for anyone else, to try to convince people of the veracity of their beliefs by simply sharing their personal experiences of those beliefs. Every person who has reached any level of maturity realizes that it is easy for us to misinterpret the meaning or significance of our experiences. For instance, five people might view an ancient piece of fabric, and while one is completely sure he sees the clear outline of the body of Jesus and is convinced he is looking at His burial shroud, the other four insist they see nothing but an old, soiled rag. History is rife with accounts of snake-oil salesmen whose worthless concoctions were reported by many users to have cured all kinds of ills, while others found no benefit in them whatsoever. Each person who used them, filtering their understanding of the experience through different expectations, desires and viewpoints, interpreted it differently. Even eyewitness testimony, though powerful evidence in courts of law, has been found to be conflicting, many times, between one eyewitness and another. It is easy to cite examples of this kind of thing.

This is not to say that experiences are never valid or that they are never to be trusted. They are quite often important personal verifications of a truth that has already begun forming in a person's mind. Knowing Christ personally is wholly experiential, but the experience is first based on a foundation of faith extrapolated from rational truth claims. No matter how profound the experience may be, or how charismatic the person who relates it, the experience belongs to that person and doesn't usually, in itself, inspire confident belief in anything for others.

And finally, the use of personal experiences, the validity of which can be known by only one person, is an unfair tactic in a propositional argument. If you're not the one who had the experience, the only way to argue against it is to effectively call your opponent a liar. So unless you're willing to do that, you're left with nothing to say.

True faith rests on the firm footing of revelation and reason. When one begins to understand truth from these sources, wonderful experiences follow. But they cannot reliably be the basis of the faith from which they spring.

Christianity versus Secular Humanism

If you compare the Christian belief system to that of secular humanism (based on atheism),[3] you see that the humanist believes that only one of these sources is sufficient for developing a correct world view—namely human reason. Because they believe there is no such thing as revelation from outside of man's mind and his physical surroundings, humanists are left to rely solely on their intellect. Absent the core truths given to us by revelation, this leads to a lack of understanding and prevents faith. To the humanist, if mankind has not objectively

To whatever degree Christianity can be called "religion," so equally can secularism in its many forms.

reasoned something out, then it either doesn't exist, hasn't yet been discovered by man, or can't be known. The irony of this position is that the humanist is right in believing that much truth can indeed be ultimately reasoned out by humans. The free and unfettered use of reason would in fact lead them to faith in divine

---

[3] The philosophy of humanism is based on a naturalistic and atheistic understanding of reality, but with an odd bent toward elevation of the human species to an almost god-like place in the order of nature. This is odd because according to naturalism, there is no warrant for a special recognition of humans. We are just another accidental species.

revelation if they would allow it. The humanists' problem is that they set arbitrary limits on their reasoning by rejecting revelation and/or the supernatural out of hand.

Please don't miss the fact that this description of secular humanism is identical to Christianity by our definition: it is a method, or system of understanding the world based on a set of presuppositions that are accepted on faith. Atheism, humanism, materialism, empiricism or any name you want to give to the various nuances of a "physical world only" philosophy are all faith-based (along with all other conceivable world views). The idea that man cannot know anything outside of the dimensions of his sensed environment can't be proved any more than a Christian can prove that the Bible accurately depicts reality. So, to whatever degree Christianity can be called "religion," so equally can secularism in its many forms.[4] So, we should begin by understanding that without exception, every belief system bases its world view on faith-based presuppositions. The trick is to find accurate ones!

Timothy Keller, in his comprehensive work *The Reason for God*, states that any world view is an implicit religion. "Broadly understood, faith in some view of the world and human nature informs everyone's life. Everyone lives and operates out of some narrative identity, whether it is thought out and reflected upon or not. All who say 'You ought to do this' or 'You shouldn't do that' reason out of such an implicit moral and religious position."[5] It doesn't matter what your view of reality entails. You are a believer in a religious faith no different in general definition than any other.

In reality, there is no such thing as a secular world view. In

---

[4] It's worth noting that if this is true, then "religion" has not been removed from U.S. schools and government. Instead, Christianity has been replaced by a different, state-supported religion.
[5] Timothy Keller, *The Reason for God* (New York: Penguin, 2008).

one way or another, we all serve some kind of god or gods. We may not bow our knee to them literally, but we certainly bow to and worship our gods in many other ways. We spend our time with them, devote ourselves to them, neglect other aspects of our life in favor of them, depend on them for happiness and fulfillment, and construct our world view around them. Whatever rules our life is our religion.

Attacks That Miss the Mark

Christianity is just one example of these systems of faith-based presuppositions about fundamental reality. It is an amazingly successful one, but regrettably, it is also one that has been misunderstood and abused over time by so many of its own, as well as by its detractors, that its reputation has been deeply wounded, as indicated in this chapter's opening questions. Throughout its history, Christianity has been confused, misrepresented, and perverted as much as any belief system that can be found among men. It has been oversimplified and overcomplicated, twisted, hijacked, misinterpreted, and used as an excuse during the entire twenty centuries of its existence. Wars and high crimes committed sadly in its name, oppressive dogma, pompous power-mongering and simply-silly iterations of its tenets have left little reason to wonder why so many find difficulty in concluding that the world view associated with Christianity is a clear and accurate "picture" of truth. Indeed, in view of similar problems with virtually all world views (including humanism/atheism, by the way), it is not surprising that so many people view truth (as in an accurate and complete understanding of their world) as incredibly difficult, if not impossible, to find.

Many atheists point to the failures of "religion" as good reason for rejecting faith. Of course, their purpose is to convince, and since they are bound only by a moral code of their own making, most don't seem to mind a little hyperbole. Although these atheists and those who quote them are usually quite off base in their understanding of the history that so appalls them, I am not really that much in disagreement with them. Religion, like all other huge, worldwide organizations, is indeed capable of, and in some cases has been responsible for, various atrocities. Recall that religion is, by one definition, an organization made up of individuals. This organization and the individuals within it are intimately involved with the people groups that are influenced by it. Of course there were and are abuses. People and organizations do that, especially if you give them enough time. More on this in chapter nine, but it suffices here to say that to reject Christianity as untrue because of the acts of those who claim it is no different than to say gravity doesn't exist because you hate Isaac Newton. It is a *non sequitur*. We are here in search of an understanding of what is true about our reality. The egregious acts of individuals and the institutions they devise, no matter what philosophy they may claim, is a symptom of their failure to understand the truth we pursue here, not a failure of that truth.

Finding the Right Path to Truth

People take various approaches to finding their world views. Most people who make any attempt at all to formulate a rational philosophy of how things really are come to a point that resembles a multi-forked junction in their progress toward an ultimate solution. There are so many voices, so many beliefs, so many possibilities, all backed up by "experts" and each with a certain level of believability, especially when presented by their most effective advocates. This is why most folks fall back to no philosophy at all, or as we've said earlier, they hold weakly to something they don't fully understand.

Over the past century and a half, the world has largely turned to science as the ultimate resolver of truth. But this has proved an empty, unsatisfying resource. Post-modern thinkers have come to the correct realization that science is limited and there are truths beyond its grasp that are important to understand. People are realizing that to fully understand the truth about reality would require a vast store of scientific, historical and philosophical knowledge. The more we learn, the more we realize that we need to learn. Because they recognize that there is so much information that exists, and will always exist, outside their own span of knowledge, and since they can't resolve the myriad complications mankind has placed on truth over time, people simply make truth up for themselves. They know that no one, no matter how capable or intelligent, can master all the disciplines necessary in order to know the truth of all matters, so they satisfy their need for a personal world view by proclaiming their own truth. Being fully aware that theirs cannot be ultimate or transcending truth because such truth can't possibly be based on the belief system of one person alone among the six-and-a-half billion people that populate the planet, they highly value respecting "everyone's truth" and then pat themselves on the back for being so enlightened. It seems like a "fair" way to go. It even feels pretty sophisticated. And it's an easy way to escape the hard work implied by a real search for truth. The sad reality though, is that because of this lack of clarity, they have long ago abandoned any real hope of fully understanding the true nature of their world.

The Role of Faith

The authentic Christian, however, is not at all post-modern. He or she accepts a world view that actually asserts an objective explanation for our presence here. Christians presuppose, as we've discussed, that all the knowledge we need to understand life has been either shared with us by a Power outside of humanity (revelation) or is accessible by means of a system of thinking created by that outside Power (logic or reason). But Christianity teaches also that these two will never be quite enough, because by God's plan, neither of these sources will ever quite disclose fully *all* truth for any specific individual. There are, and will continue to be, many tough questions about what is fundamentally true about our reality. Even C. S. Lewis, the great defender of Christianity, spent much time juxtaposing his confident apologetics against the thorny questions that lack easy answers. There will always be some truth that is unrevealed, undiscovered, or in some cases, beyond human reasoning. In truth, we should celebrate this fact rather than lamenting it. It is in man's best interest to know that there is an Entity outside himself on which he can rely for handling the truths that he will never discover or the nuances and implications of truth that he will never develop fully. This type of dependency is one of the inborn needs created in us. Philosophers have recognized the universal human need that we have for interdependent relationships with each other. To be healthy and to function effectively in our world, we need to be dependent on others to meet our various higher-level needs.[6] We will not be fulfilled, optimized human beings if we attempt to remain self-contained. To know with confidence that the world is orderly and that certain truths can be relied upon is one of our higher-level human needs. But we cannot meet that

> *It is in man's best interest to know that there is an Entity outside himself on which he can rely for handling the truths that he will never discover*

---

[6] See A. Maslow, *Toward a Psychology of Being* (New York: D. Van Nostrand Co., 1954, 1968), et al.

nagging need by turning solely to other humans, because they exist in the same state as we do, unable to resolve the truth of all matters. Christians believe that on those matters that we can't quite reach with our human intellect, we must trust the revelations that God has given us, including His assurance that He knows what we don't and that He is in control of what we cannot manage.

This faith requires submitting to the authority of scripture. So much of what the Christian faith relies on is contained there that, without it, the belief system becomes an empty, meaningless human tradition. Medieval philosopher Thomas Aquinas (ca. 1225-1274) explained the Christian's faith in a three-step process:

First, as we'll develop more fully in chapter five, he said that *fulfilled prophecy* and *miracles* make credible the idea that the Bible is a revelation from God (and I would add *historical accuracy*, something Aquinas didn't have the benefit of knowing much about). Second, if scripture is indeed a revelation from the kind of Creator-God discussed in these pages, then it is, by any reasonable logic, absolutely authoritative. Third, the doctrines and ideas that are presented in scripture that can't be verified or are not empirically evident to humankind must be accepted on faith in the authority of scripture. Thus, Aquinas would say that a reasonable person should be convinced of the truths Christians hold by faith on the basis of the authority of scripture as confirmed by the prophecy and miracles (and historical accuracy) contained in it.[7]

I've read some atheists to whom this methodology (and the idea of faith in general) is an example of one of their best-worn criticisms of Christianity—the famous "God-of-the-gaps"

---

[7] Aquinas' analysis paraphrased from W. L. Craig, *Reasonable Faith: Christian Truth and Apologetics*, 2nd edition (Wheaton, IL: Crossway Books, 2008).

complaint. Basically, this disparagement alleges that when Christians or other religious folk come upon a problem or situation that they can't fully explain given their world view, they simply cop out by saying "God did it," or "God will resolve it." A more accurate way to put it would be that Christians view faith as an acceptable place to rest their uncertainty when facing this kind of question. It is understandable that this sort of answer is frustrating to materialists, who think there should be a physical answer or proof for everything. Their complaint—an understandable one—is that such an answer cuts off debate. How can anyone formulate an argument against that? But for one who believes in the Creator-God described in this book, this would have to be a fair response when questions reach beyond the understanding of limited mankind. After all, our whole belief system is based on the belief in One who is far more powerful and knowledgeable than ourselves.

Such a response is certainly as reasonable as the common atheist one that says, "We don't know the answer to that problem yet, but one day science will find it." As an example of this, someone has famously said, "Cosmology is waiting for its Darwin." In other words, if we don't know some critical answers in the field of cosmology, well, just wait; human intellect will one day find these answers. When a materialist cannot explain something, he too responds, out of faith in his world view, that a natural explanation will one day be found, or, as is more often the case, he will formulate some sort of fanciful theory and advance it as fact, often knowing full well that it is not. These are expressions of *faith* in a belief system just as surely as is the so-called God-of-the-gaps response. Both could be fairly dubbed a "Belief-System-of-the-Gaps" response.

> *Where man's intellect fails, faith begins.*

A mature Christian understands that God has said to us, in essence, *I have given you a mind powerful enough to take you beyond mere facts, and enough information to form the correct conclusion that you will never know everything that I know, so you must trust Me.* This faith, then, is the final element essential to a proper understanding of the reason for our existence and one of the keys to unlocking fulfillment in our lives. Faith is the glue that holds it all together. Where man's intellect fails, faith begins. Where there is no revealed truth on a matter, faith provides a place to which the mind can turn. Without it, man is left to his own, highly limited resources. God values mankind's efforts at discovering answers. In fact, it's my belief that He delights in them. But man's knowledge can never approach that of an all-knowing God. No matter how much man learns, it will always be necessary for him to accept by faith that God is in control of the things he doesn't yet fully understand. To be a fulfilled human being, man must add faith to the two sources of truth. He must accept that he is a limited creature and that he must depend on, or have faith in, the One who is unlimited.

So Christianity, when stripped of the burden of man's folly, can be thought of as a way of illuminating, as the line from the movie *Casualties of War* puts it, "the terrain in which we currently find ourselves deployed." Through the conduits of revelation and reason and with the support of a reasoned faith, we have everything that we need to understand the physical world, as well as what lies outside of that realm, at least to the degree necessary to fulfill our planned destiny—to commune with, serve and love the Creator of everything. Neither we nor our world will be perfect or without trials in the present thanks to our own choices, but the more we seek truth from all the sources God has made available to us, the more we will understand about our reality, and the more joy, contentment, and satisfaction we will experience.

The Spiritual Realm

Of course, there is more to Christianity than simply establishing a correct world view. We have been discussing so far the intellectual side of the Christian experience. This *revelation* part of the equation (the Bible) tells us of another plane of existence, another world outside our own from which our Creator comes and to which He goes. More accurately, He exists in both realms simultaneously. While our *self*, or our soul, is locked in our bodies, we can exist primarily in only one realm. But though we are, for the moment, bound to the physical world, we are not insensitive to the spiritual one. God has created us capable of sensing, interacting with and communing with the spiritual realm, and has sent a form of Himself to live among us, prompt us, teach us and comfort us. I will cover this more fully in chapter eight. Ultimately, we will move to that other realm where we will be perfectly happy, perfectly content and fulfilled beyond our imagination for all eternity.

The Freedom to Choose

There is, however, another, less pleasant possibility for our ultimate future, and we must choose which we prefer. Because of a thing called *love* (a human capability that reflects our likeness of Him), God has abdicated the power to make that choice for us. He will not force His creation to choose an eternity with Him. He loves those He has made in His image enough to make them free to choose what they will. Since the creation, millions have gone their own way, and not only suffered the consequences of their choices but also placed their progeny and those under their influence under the weight of their arrogance, strongly influencing them toward the same fate.

But in God's perfect time and according to His perfect plan, He sent a form of Himself, embodied in human likeness and fully human like each of us, to remove the barrier we had placed between ourselves and Him, so that we would be fully free to make our choice.[8] There will be more about this God-man in chapter seven.

Christians call this story of free choice the *gospel*.

Can something like that be real? Is it possible with our limited understanding to know that a world outside our five senses actually exists? With the open mind of an honest inquirer, the answer is a compelling yes. In fact, we know it already. The preceding pages have tried to show how every human life begins with an intrinsic understanding of and belief in this truth. Even humanists, as I've said, who discount the idea of revelation and faith, relying only on human reason, still have the capacity to understand that this world outside of nature *must* exist. Many in fact do understand this. But since they reject the revelation of scripture and have no faith in its God, they end up with many odd and bizarre explanations of this spiritual realm which they realize must be there.[9]

So, this is the essence of the world view, or belief system, called Christianity. It is not the ritual behavior, or lack of it, seen on Sunday and other days at any church. That's just the form established mostly by men as a way of honoring and worshiping the Creator God in whom Christians and others believe. Obviously, Christian forms of worship vary greatly. One can

---

[8] Note that this truth can only be understood because it has been *revealed* in scripture. Man could not have reached this truth through the use of his own intellect, and because to our limited minds it seems to have mysterious aspects, we must accept it by faith. Humanism/atheism rejects this truth because it rejects revelation as a source of truth.

[9] Note that such explanations originate from the imagination of man, which is not one of the sources of truth. Examples in Western culture would be mysticism, transcendentalism, new age beliefs, spiritualism, scientology and any number of post-modern ideas.

choose the form that suits his personality, and that in his mind and heart best expresses the revealed truth of scripture. But the truth itself never varies.

Nor is Christianity the acts, whether good or bad, of religious institutions or religious individuals. Christianity is the truth about reality.

If one looks honestly and openly to the two sources of truth; revelation and reason, placing his faith in the Author of them, and allows no one to lead him into man's perverse imaginations which originate outside of these sources, then he can know the truth. As G. K. Chesterton implies in the quote opening this chapter, it's not always easy. The fulfillment comes in the trying.

Chapter Four

Who Is God, and Why Do So Many Disagree about Him?

"Thou Great First Cause, least understood, who all my sense confined to know but this; that Thou art good, and I myself am blind…"
—*Alexander Pope*

Humankind has been seeking to know the specific attributes of whatever god or gods may exist throughout recorded history. Almost as many expressions of Him (or them) have been offered and devoutly believed in as there have been people groups throughout the ages. There have been multiple, human-like gods who interact with and even marry humans. God has often been viewed as a pervasive spirit without personhood or form. There have been celestial objects deified and worshipped, as well as just about any natural object, whether animate or not. The planet earth has been imbued with a god-spirit of its own, and life itself has been given god-like qualities. Today, we are still left with a number of differing views about who God is and what His attributes are. In view of this, *why should the Christian view of God be accepted as more accurate than any one of the others?* This is certainly a reasonable question asked by critics and seekers alike. In fact, it is more than just reasonable. We are born with a compulsion to find its answer. But before considering this question, we should first answer a more basic one: How, over time, have various cultures come up with so many different expressions and characterizations of this Creator God in whom our natural impulses lead us to believe?

Going back to basics again, Christianity, like all world views, bases its thinking on certain presuppositions. As I continue to point out, there is no such thing as a "pure" world view based solely on empirical data, so the key to developing an accurate view of reality is to stand it upon the strong foundation of the most logically supportable presuppositions available. The single most important presupposition of the Christian world view is that the collection of scriptures known as the Bible presents the true history of the world and that its accounts are inspired, controlled and preserved by the one eyewitness of all history—the God in whom we believe. Christians believe that the Bible lays out the only accurate description of the Creator God, what His attributes are, His character and his plan for us. Christendom counts this presupposition reliable for many powerful and satisfying reasons.

The key to developing an accurate view of reality is to stand it upon the strong foundation of the most logically supportable presuppositions.

Of course, like any claim about unrepeatable events in bygone eras, the veracity of every statement in the Bible cannot be proved in the scientific sense. But as mankind's knowledge has increased over the ages, our new discoveries have always been consistent with what has been written down in the text we know as the Bible. This cannot be said about the vast majority of the speculations and suppositions of man. Theories and hypotheses change with every wind of new discovery. But the Bible has never changed. Rather than new information coming along and correcting it, the Bible is consistent with and sheds light on new information that arises in mankind's search for knowledge. It is incredible to think that so many different authors writing over such a long and ancient span of time wrote down not one word that can be shown inaccurate today. This includes statements about the physical world that could not have been known to the writers at the time. Yet much of mankind continues to insist that a world view based on its own ever-changing ideas is more reliable.

The Only Accurate History of the Ancient World

The next chapter will expand on the reasons for placing faith in God's word, but for now, we're going to proceed on the assumption that the Bible can be trusted, as Christians should, and look to the true history found in it to understand why God has been seen and worshipped in so many different ways by so many different cultures. Actually, there is no other place to look for this information. If you think about it, no other document, philosophy, or belief system purports to explain why so much of mankind has been confused over the true nature of God for so long a time. But in reading the Bible, one finds woven into the powerful accounts of creation and God's people the true historical backdrop of events that led to these misunderstandings. The modern problem is that as man has been digging up fossils, discovering radioactive decay rates[1] and

---

[1] The idea of discovering the ages of things by radiometric dating has many fatal flaws. Using it to determine that the earth is billions of years old is an example of the wishful thinking of determined humanists and is bad science in general. More on this in chapter nine.

analyzing rock strata, few have based their findings and hypotheses on the only written history of the world's beginnings. Had they done so with an open mind, they would have been awe-stricken by the complete consistency of what we find today with what ancient men wrote thousands of years ago.

This history teaches clearly that less than two thousand years after creation, the curse of original sin had affected man so profoundly that he could do nothing but evil continually, so God judged mankind by sending a flood to cover the entire earth (an earth very different from the one we know today) for the purpose of killing all land-dwelling, air-breathing life, save the eight members of one righteous family and a small sampling of each of His created kinds of animals. The belief that this account of the greatest catastrophe in recorded history is true is highly defensible intellectually and supported by much evidence found all over the world today, not the least of which are the presence of marine fossils on many of the mountaintops of the world and the existence of myriad layers of sedimentary rock, sometimes extending unbroken across entire continents and containing fossils of countless creatures entombed suddenly in some unexpected event. A song often used by a popular ministry supporting Biblical creation puts it this way:

> "If there really was a worldwide flood, what would the evidence be? Billions of dead things buried in rock layers laid down by water, all over the earth!"[2]

Well, if one presupposes that the Bible is true, that is indeed what he would expect to find. Oddly (in the view of secular

---

[2] Buddy Davis, *Billions of Dead Things* (Petersburg, KY: Answers In Genesis), www.answersingenesis.com.

science), that is exactly what we do find. In fact, the earth's geology is a screaming testament to the truth of the flood account and the veracity of God's word.[3] This is why denying the idea of a worldwide flood is so essential to the agenda of atheist scientists. The truth, though, is that this is what we find with all historical accounts found in the Bible—they are fully reasonable in light of current knowledge if not rejected *a priori*.[4]

So there really was a flood that covered the whole earth, a catastrophe of epic proportions, and after it subsided, the remnant of man and animal kind inhabited a new world, vastly changed from the one they knew.

The Effects of the Great Flood

During the flood year, God had repainted His earth in a new expression of His creative power. As the earth gave up its subterranean water stores,[5] continental plates broke apart, slid (possibly on a lubricating layer of water) and came to sudden, crushing stops in various places against the underlying mantle. Great mountain ranges were formed by the crushing, over-thrusting and bending of impossibly huge masses of rock, while megatons of sediment were distributed over them by the flood waters. Over the following centuries, these colossal land masses settled haltingly into their final resting places, being moved, sunken and raised by the geologic forces begun by the flood. The remnants of this greatest friction event of all history give us

---

[3] Truly a fulfillment of Jesus' prophecy in Luke 19:40: "…if these men keep quiet, the very stones will be crying out." The earth's geology is "crying out" in testimony to the truth of God's word in an age when men will not do so.

[4] The idea of a flood covering the entire earth raises many questions. If you would like more answers, see www.answersingenesis.org/arj (which has many rigorous scientific analyses of the flood record) or go to www.creationresearch.org or www.worldwideflood.com.

[5] Genesis 7:11.

much of the volcanism, earthquakes and other geological activity we see today. But in the first few centuries following the flood, molten crustal material oozing and bursting from the earth must have been the norm in many places. In fact, it is likely that an ash cloud covered most of the earth for decades or even centuries, which, together with the warm oceans created by this incredible geological activity, was a critical element in causing the ice age.

Because of the strong influence of current naturalist thought, many who read the foregoing paragraph will be incredulous of the idea that all of this happened in a relatively short time during and after the great flood. Yet all geological and other evidence, when looked at through the eyeglass of scripture, points to a scenario something like this, and there is no known, responsible science that can refute it. So it is a reasonable hypothesis, given the evidence seen through the glasses of scripture. Do we *know* in an empirical sense that this is what happened? No, of course not. Neither Christians nor secularists were there, and neither the Bible nor the evidence left today describe fully how the geology of the earth reached its present state. So we can only construct reasoned speculations. However, changing this hypothesis of the earth's geological history to one of uniformitarian processes over billions of years and numerous ice ages does nothing to establish its veracity. Arriving at such a hypothesis merely requires putting on your "no god, no flood" glasses and interpreting the evidence in that light. The difference is one of world view, not one of evidence. Christianity chooses to presuppose that the amazing record provided for us by the infallible God of creation

> *Christianity chooses to presuppose that the amazing record provided for us by the infallible God of creation is a better basis for theorizing than fallible mankind's imagination.*

is a better basis for theorizing than fallible mankind's imagination. Again, we'll talk more about why this is a reasonable presupposition in the next chapter.

The unparalleled catastrophe of the great flood did eventually subside. The remnant of man and animal kind survived, and over the ensuing years, began to proliferate.

The Scattering of Mankind over the Earth

God commanded the budding population to disperse and populate the whole earth, but in mankind's usual way, people ignored the command, and over the next few generations, they stayed close together in one area, apparently a rich plain, as the population re-grew. Fearful of striking out, they lived there, working to build a new life over about the next eleven decades, everyone speaking the same language and putting to use all the knowledge gained since the creation to build a great city. The Bible records that they decided to build a majestic tower as a unifying factor for the new culture, so that they would remain united as one people and not scatter over the earth, thus revealing an opposite motivation to the command they had been given. This is just one story in the unbroken litany of examples of man believing that what he reasons for himself should overrule the reasoning of his Creator. The tower became a monument to their commitment to disobedience. Apparently, even the disaster of disasters, the great flood, wasn't enough to dissuade Noah's descendents from ignoring their God.

Knowing that the opportunity to populate the entire earth would be limited due to the continuing changes in earth's geology in the next several centuries to come, God imposed His will on men by compelling them to speak different languages for the first time in history.[6] Confused and frustrated by the sudden inability

---

[6] See Genesis 11:1-9.

to understand anyone but those of their own small language group, the groups separated from each other and began roaming the earth looking for a place in which to flourish. If only man could learn that God's purposes cannot be thwarted.

The Apparent Primitiveness of Early Man

If you take the evidence of early peoples we find today and compare it to this Biblical description of the dispersion of people-groups at the tower of Babel, it is easy to infer from it that relatively small people-groups became, in effect, exiled to various parts of the world, creating genetic bottlenecks and isolating technical knowledge in different locations. Instead of dreaming up wild stories about "ape men" and a "stone age" and so forth, modern mankind could have simply read the history and seen what happened. Some of these isolated people-groups may have wandered for centuries looking for a better environment, making use of the land bridges that likely still connected the continents and the ice bridges of the *one*[7] ice age caused by the aftereffects of the flood; along the way, they may have left behind even smaller isolated groups. Some groups would have possessed much of the knowledge of the larger post-flood society; some would have become primitive because of the lack of such knowledge (and accordingly, lived in caves when they were available). This is why we find such a wide variety of ancient cultures. The historicity of this forced-dispersion story, like that of the flood, is consistent with modern evidence and scholarship. For instance, studies of the geographic history of languages appears to trace them all back to the general area of Mesopotamia, which is thought to be the cradle of post-flood civilization. Moreover, we find a great deal of evidence that some ancient cultures were not as primitive as our

---

[7] M. Oard, *An Ice Age Caused by the Genesis Flood* (Dallas: Institute for Creation Research, 2002).

educational programming leads us to believe. We find evidence all over the world of societies that appear to have understood many things that our vanity has led us to assume we were the first to know. Several cultures apparently understood our solar system to a high degree of accuracy; many were outstanding architects and builders, in some cases astounding us with the massive, intricately fitted stone structures that we find today in many places; some, thousands of years ago, apparently knew of and harnessed electricity and constructed complicated mechanical computers.[8] At the same time, many were struggling and isolated, resorting to crude techniques to support basic survival because their language group lacked technical knowledge and their geographic location presented them with severe obstacles to their survival. Here again, history and scholarship, when fully understood, always support the Biblical accounts.

The history of mankind given in the Bible up until the tower of Babel was the story of the whole of mankind, because the human species at that time lived relatively close to one another. They were all one people group. Until the flood, there was only one land mass,[9] and man had never had a notable incentive to wander. After Babel, when mankind was split into different groups because of language barriers, the Bible history began to follow a particular people-group in whom God chose to entrust His story. There was only one history being written at this time, fortunately an infallibly accurate one, and by the Creator's choice, it recorded one group's history. We know a great deal

---

[8] It's almost embarrassing to watch the many "documentaries" on television and read them in magazines attributing these achievements to contact with aliens! This is the best secular mankind can do to maintain consistency with their unsound view of ancient history.

[9] Genesis 1:9. *"God gathered the waters into one place."* Hence, the dry land was also in one place. This is consistent with current secular understanding of geology that implies an original single land mass, dubbed "Pangea."

about this chosen people and a little about some of the groups that interacted with them over time, but of the other groups, we know only what the evidence we find in the present implies. To the atheist, this evidence implies that there were forerunner versions of our species, and a Darwinian mindset leads to stories of multiple branches of pre-human species leading to the various races of modern man. To the Christian, seeing it through Biblical glasses, it implies that some groups of God's highest creation survived and thrived while some suffered illnesses or encountered hardships that affected their genetic makeup, and in some cases, even led to their extinction as a group.[10] A clear view of this history also leads us to understand that mankind is divided into what we call "races" over the miniscule genetic differences caused by the combination of genetic isolation and environmental influences. If we understood this history clearly, it would be easy to see that in fact we are all of the same "race" —the human one.

The Origin of Conflicting Religions

In the same way, if one accepts the Bible's account as Christianity does and views the issue of competing religions in its light, it isn't hard to see how the understanding of God among diverse people groups became varied. The Bible doesn't record what happened to the various groups, but it's reasonable to expect that any given group, once separated from the whole, would possess among its members only a partial understanding

---

[10] It may be important to note here, and I will discuss this more later, that *natural selection* is a process that is not disputed by the vast majority of creation believers. Christians do understand that species' change (including the human species) due to genetic and environmental pressures. Due to specific genetic limitations, however, one created *kind* of creature cannot change into a completely different kind. The ancient humans referenced here were all human, never apes. Apes are and always were a separate *kind*, and all fossil evidence to date supports that fact.

of the history of God's interaction with man, just as it would possess only a partial pool of the larger population's genes, or only a portion of its technical knowledge. The accuracy and completeness of the collective memory regarding God in any of these isolated societies would vary based on which members of the former whole were captured into that language group. Moreover, this level of accuracy would likely decrease with time as verbal records were handed down by imperfect human memories. In any given language group, caretakers of the historical record, at least for several generations, would have been few because such a pursuit would have seemed trivial compared to the daily battle to survive in an unfamiliar part of an ever-changing world. In addition, the verbal records would soon have succumbed to human nature as they were re-shaped by those who sought to use them to gain power and influence over others.

In other words, knowledge of the reality of a supernatural Creator-God was present in all post-Babel cultures, but details were lost, obscured, and deliberately distorted with time. This is why God chose a particular people group in whom to vest an accurate, written history of the early earth. Moving chosen individuals to write down His history, He set the record straight permanently, and over time, He charged the keepers of this history with the responsibility of sharing it with the rest of mankind. This history, of course, is only a small part of what God had to say to us through those to whom he revealed His word. It would have done mankind no good to merely have an eyewitness record of the history of the earth. If God had stopped there, we could not have known Him fully. Happily for us, His word also records

Human beings are born with an innate belief in, understanding of and need for God.

who He is, how we can know Him personally, why He made us and what His plan is for us.

So, the post-flood dispersion of mankind over the earth and the loss of connection between the various people groups answer the basic question of why, over time, we have had these many different expressions and characterizations of this God who, we know from our birth, must exist. Although nature was always intended to be only an expression of the character and power of the Creator God, some groups, over time, began to revere the created elements of their environment *as* god, rather than *of* God. In addition, and again over dozens of centuries, individuals arose in various cultures claiming to have received personal revelations from God, or from *a* god or *the* gods, in accordance with what they believed their culture might accept. Occasionally, they even claimed to *be* a god, or to be God's sole chosen intermediary with mankind. This continues from time to time to this day.

There is another important point to be made about the rise of confusion over God across the centuries. One might reasonably ask, why wouldn't the various people groups, in their struggle for survival, just forget about the idea of God over time? Why would they need to keep characterizing Him, defining Him and maintaining some form of belief in Him? The answer is found in what we've already discussed—human beings are born with an innate belief in, understanding of and need for God. These so-called "primitive" peoples were no different than we are. They deeply needed to know who their Creator was, and how they could relate to Him.

It Could Have Been Different

It should be pointed out, before moving on, that this confusion and loss of information about God was not necessary, nor was it God's perfect plan.[11] Mankind could have spared itself the inconceivable number of lost souls caused by this loss of knowledge had it simply obeyed the direction of the most intelligent and powerful Entity imaginable. But as has been the case so often in history (and in each of our personal histories), man thought himself wiser than God and huddled together in one place against God's command. The world had to be populated while the opportunity existed, and had the first generation following the flood done as commanded, they could have carried with them a fresh and accurate record of creation, the flood, and the true nature of God as they roamed the changed planet. They could have taken with them all of the technology and knowledge of the original group, thereby avoiding the need to resort to a primitive lifestyle, and sometimes, even the extinction of their group. They might have maintained the ability to communicate back and forth between groups in the same language, thus preserving a more correct view of the Creator. As it happened, though, the God of creation, ever patient and tolerating their disobedience until it could be tolerated no longer, forced their compliance. As a result, many groups over time were left without members who could provide them with an accurate record of Him.

So, we are left today with many myths and traditions, many of them grounded in truth but perverted by time or added to by the imagination of man. If one can imagine a thing, then it has at some point in history been added to or has replaced the true story of the Creation and human history. As I continually point out, man's imagination is never a source of truth, and the person who learns to separate revelation and solid reasoning from

---

[11] As we'll see later, God does not change His mind. The fact that God knew how things should have worked (His perfect plan) doesn't mean that He changed His plan. All of His plans will ultimately be realized, and for Him, there are no surprises along the way.

man's imagination is the person who is capable of knowing the truth about God.

A Modern Resurgence of a Universal Need

But it is not only the person and the attributes of God that the human race is confused about. It is the nature of the supernatural itself. In late-modern times, and to varying degrees throughout our history, we have been regaled with many distortions of spirituality in general. Today we have spiritualists, card readers, palm readers, mediums, seers, mystics, healers, pantheists, theosophists, occultists and countless others who claim some special understanding of the supernatural world. We are fervently informed of the reality of animal spirit guides, vortices, reincarnation, ghosts, contacts with departed loved ones, visions of future events and any number of other spiritual oddities. Many intelligent and reasonable individuals believe wholeheartedly in these various forms of modern spirituality and ardently cling to them.

I submit to you that this trend in our culture is understandable and predictable. As I have tried to show, man has two natures. The supernatural man is every bit as real and far more enduring than the physical one. Every person has an inborn need to express himself or herself spiritually. This inner voice wishes to speak, and if it is silenced, it cries out to be heard. For the better part of two centuries now, our species

> *The supernatural man is every bit as real and far more enduring than the physical one.*

has been indoctrinated more and more in the idea that the physical world is the sum total of our reality. Secularism in its various nuances has slowly but surely lowered the heavy lid of naturalism over the warm cauldron of our congenital spirituality. We have been programmed to suppress any urge to allow the possibility of a reality outside of nature because such an idea has been so effectively sold as parochial, unsophisticated and ignorant. For so long, we have marched in lock step with so-called intellectualism, afraid that the slightest misstep toward spirituality will cost us our place on the modern bandwagon of thought.

But under the tight lid of naturalism, the kettle of human spirituality has come to a boil. The aroma of something cooking—something that might be real and satisfying and sustaining—cannot be ignored. The need that percolates beneath the popular thought of our self-styled sophisticates has boiled over, and it escapes and explodes in undirected and chaotic expressions of our inborn need for understanding of our eternal selves—the souls that will exist for all eternity.

We have raised several generations of people who have never been given any sort of rational guidance about how to express their spirituality. The powerful force of popular opinion has kept this need under wraps, and as they reach maturity, these children of Darwin are exploding with longing to know what else there is. Like blind archers firing at every sound, they follow any philosophy that seems to present the remotest possibility of spiritual fulfillment. *God? Well yes, there probably is one, but traditional religious views of Him have led to nothing but problems (so says my spiritualist). I'll seek Him in my own way.* If this generation thinks of attending church at all, it gravitates toward those that extend only feel-good philosophizing about some ethereal god who is on their side but never interferes with their choices or beliefs, or asks anything of them. They would never think of slipping into a traditional church pew to see if there are any real and satisfying answers there. Such is the great success of modern secularism, humanism, atheism, naturalism and theological liberalism. And sadly, it is the great failure of the contemporary Christian church.

The Nature of the Christian God

The difference between the one true God, who is sought and served by authentic Christianity, and other traditions about a god or gods, or about spirituality in general, is that the Christian God is the God of the Bible. The Bible is the record of what God wants us to know, at least as a starting point about Him and about our history with Him. No other record that stands up to the scrutiny of history tells the complete story. Looking to the Bible to understand the totality of our reality is the only rational approach to the issue.

The Bible describes this God as an entity that exists outside of time, because He is the creator of it. He is "omnipresent," meaning that there is no place within His creation where He is absent at any time.[12] It should go without saying that since He has created all things, He knows all there is to know about all things; He is "omniscient."[13] We have a personal God, who speaks to us on many levels[14] and is capable of having a relationship with us.[15] Yet He is an awesome God, wielding unlimited power at his will.[16] In chapter six, I'll expand upon another attribute of God; His justice.

Most importantly, the Bible reveals that God is perfect. When referring to the spiritual or moral aspect of perfection, the Bible often calls this attribute "holiness."[17] What this means, simply, is that God is morally error-free in all He does. It is His nature, and as such, He cannot deny Himself by communing with error. Moral error, called sin in the Bible, is what keeps us

---

[12] Psalm 139:7-12.
[13] Isaiah 40:14 & 28.
[14] One of many examples: Acts 13:2.
[15] I John 1:3.
[16] Isaiah 50:2.
[17] Isaiah 6:3.

separated from Him.

If we, as God's special creation, could only adopt the attitude expressed by the great English poet Alexander Pope in the opening quotation of this chapter, it would be the most significant step we might take in developing a right relationship with our Creator. If we could simply internalize the idea that He is good, and we are blind, we might accept more easily the things that He has told us, and might thereby begin meeting the aching need in every man for an understanding of the true nature of things and for a relationship with Him.

The Bible is our source of *revelation*, which is the only place we find truth from outside of our own intellect. It is the benchmark by which the Christian measures truth. While nearly every culture and "religion" on earth has traditional stories about creation, a flood or floods, language confusion, and even a "savior" figure, no culture has the whole truth unless it has, and accepts as true, the scripture that God has given and preserved through the ages. This chapter and the previous one assumed that this great book commands our trust. The next chapter will support that assumption.

Chapter Five

Why Can the Christian Bible Be Trusted over Other Religious Writings?

*"The Bible is the Cradle
Wherein Christ is Laid."*
—*Martin Luther*

To restate one of the main themes of this book, beliefs and belief systems have to be based on *something*. The human mind cannot pull a critical belief about reality out of a vacuum (although it sometimes seems so). Because we are not God and don't possess all of His attributes, and because we were not present at the beginning of time and throughout history, we cannot discover during our time any empirical truth about our reality and how it came to be. It is not possible because we were not there to see the establishment of this reality, and in our day, we have only the effective results of several thousand years to look at. So whatever historical science calls "truth" about how things really are is actually an estimation of what the truth *may be*, based on what the scientist currently sees and limited by his knowledge and the biases his world view imposes on it. Again—present evidence of a bygone reality seen through the glasses of presupposition. And as pointed out in chapter one, we have no choice but to assume that certain foundational beliefs (such as *first principals*) are true before we can proceed to understand the life that we experience in the present. Those first chapters also showed that a foundational degree of understanding about reality is programmed into us by our Creator and how these basic tools for building an understanding of life can only lead to a naturalist world view if naturalist principals are disregarded![1]

Clearly, the Christian belief system chooses to accept the Bible as the basis for its understanding of how things really are. Christians believe that it is the correct assumption, or presupposition, on which to base our thinking. We believe this initially because it comports with our internally programmed understanding of life, and our belief is confirmed as we apply reason to the question. However, others choose to accept materialism, naturalism and the like, with their rejection of any god, while still others choose any one of dozens of belief systems that allow for some kind of deity or some degree of spirituality. But to arrive at transcendent truth, one must start with something. If you presuppose nothing, you get nowhere, because your search is hampered by your limited human mind and the lack of the empirical evidence[2] needed to find an empirical solution.

One who is a Christian, though, has accepted that there is only one plausible collection of documents that records eyewitness and inspired accounts of how things got to be the

---

[1] Refer back to chapter one to review why this is true.

[2] It could be argued that evidence found in the present is empirical in the sense that it can be seen, touched and measured, but such measurement can only shed light on the characteristics of the evidence, not on how it came to be the way it is. When a hypothesis is formed about what happened to place the evidence where it is or what forces caused it to have its current characteristics, a researcher moves from the empirical to the speculative.

way they are and what that means to us as humans. Talk to Christians the world over and you will find hundreds and thousands of differing testimonies about what finally convinced each person to resolve that Biblical Christianity held the correct world view. But ultimately, each one of them must have come to realize that any given person's mind alone cannot reach a full understanding of their existence, and so they accepted what they were convinced is, at least in large degree,[3] the one true account. If you look at the Bible with the open mind of a true scholar and seek out a full understanding of what it says and the claims it makes, you will see that Christians accept it for good reason.

The Bible's Secular Reputation

Of course, the whole business of having an open mind is almost always a problem. On any given day, one doesn't have to search the media for too long to find tendentious comments about all aspects of faith, the Bible being no exception. They are everywhere. Those who would eliminate God from the culture, and who believe they can rule their own lives sell nonsense about the Bible's contents and history as self-evident truth.

Everywhere, you hear that the Bible is a collection of stories told by mostly ignorant, ancient nomads.

And they do it with malice and great energy. It is hard to understand why it is so important for atheists to attack other beliefs. One would think that since they believe nothing

---

[3] Many Christians question parts of the Bible. Questioning a straightforward, natural meaning of scripture is a privilege arising from the freedom given to us by our Creator, but it is logically fallacious because for a Christian, it creates serious internal conflict within the belief system, and those who hold a view like this open themselves to many valid attacks on the veracity of their faith. But this alone, of course, does not bring into question their genuine faith in Christ.

(regarding God), it would be unimportant what others believe. For them, it should be like arguing against the Easter bunny—not worth spending a lot of time on. One can only guess that vocal atheists may suffer from a syndrome taught to me when I was very young and repeated when I studied logic: The volume and vitriol of an argument is often inversely proportional to the confidence of its defender.

Everywhere, you hear that the Bible is a collection of stories told by mostly ignorant, ancient nomads. If you believe the loudest of the arguments out there, you believe that the Bible is riddled with contradictions and that many of its claims have been proven false by modern science and various discoveries. Important writings have been eliminated from the canon because they relate histories very different from what we see in traditional scripture. Skim any of the recent books by the new atheists aimed at discrediting religion (or more specifically, God) and you will not have to go too many pages in to find such claims. But an open and seeking mind will find that such claims are based not on fact but on shallow reading, weak understanding of the texts and the history that surrounds them and an agenda hostile to the Christian narrative. These prejudicial claims are canards that are wished true by many arrogant humans and are therefore easily believed and repeated. And they are often grounded in the presupposition that any account claiming supernatural events should be given no weight. Deep and honest inquiry, however, reveals that the opposites of these claims are actually true.

An Amazing Book

As mentioned briefly in the previous chapter, the Bible is an ancient document that maintains a truly remarkable resiliency over time. Surely those who tend to believe that it is an unimportant collection of legends handed down by nomads cannot name another compilation of documents written by at least forty different authors living in different eras, and never updated, corrected, or "brought in line with current thinking," that stands up to every new wave of human discovery and many systematic attempts to undermine or eliminate it and has never been found wrong[4] in any way! Think of it. The Bible was written over a sixteen-hundred-year span, and not a word has been added for two thousand more. It touches on not only spiritual things but on geology (creation, the flood, curvature of the earth, movement of continents and other references),[5] biology (the origin of life and different people-groups, "life is in the blood" and other references),[6] astronomy ("He made the stars also," He "hung the earth upon nothing," expansion of space, the uniqueness of the earth etc.),[7] anthropology (dispersion at Babel, implying the reason for early isolation of people groups and their apparent primitiveness),[8] physics, (conservation of mass and energy),[9] thermodynamics (entropy),[10] and meteorology (weather patterns and the hydrologic cycle of water),[11] among others. These facts of nature are not stated in scientific terms, of course, but are accurately stated in terms every person can understand. The important point is that they are *completely consistent* with everything we have discovered. Modern science can find nothing to dispute the record of more than three dozen ancient, unrelated men who had no access to today's discoveries. They spoke of things they couldn't have known were it not for the inspiration of the

---

[4] Accused, certainly, but never proved wrong once all evidence is fully understood.
[5] Genesis 1 and 2, Isaiah 40:22.
[6] Genesis 1 and 11, Leviticus 17:11.
[7] Genesis 1:16, Job 26:7, Isaiah 40:22, Isaiah 45:18.
[8] Genesis 11:1-9.
[9] II Peter 3:7.
[10] Psalm 102:25-27.
[11] Ecclesiastes 1:6,7.

Creator Himself. And in an age when little was known about the earth and incorrect assumptions about the physical world abounded, these writers never repeated one erroneous belief of their time!

Furthermore, these men who wrote for different reasons across three continents and in three languages never contradicted one another. Of course they are accused of it, but even if one were to accept whatever disputed claims there may be about a passage here or there contradicting another,[12] there is still a strong and pervasive consistency and unity of message that only the most optimistic of fools would expect under such circumstances apart from the guidance of a supreme, transcendent intelligence. This amazing compilation of writings remains, more than two thousand years after its completion, the world's runaway bestseller. It's ironic that this incredible book predicted even the foolishness of those who find nothing in it to amaze them.[13]

It's true there are many other religious documents that put forth a world view of their own, some claiming divine inspiration.

> *This amazing compilation of writings remains, more than two thousand years after its completion, the world's runaway bestseller.*

There are the Vedas and the Upanishads of Hinduism, the Pali Canon of Buddhism, the Book of Mormon and Pearl of Great Price, the Qur'an and many others. But none of these begin to approach the mind-boggling consistency, unity, prophecy, accuracy and power of the Bible.

The following are just a few examples.

---

[12] Which I do not.
[13] Romans 1:21,22; *For although they knew God, they neither glorified him as God nor gave thanks to him, but their thinking became futile and their foolish hearts were darkened. Although they claimed to be wise, they became fools.*

Donald R. Wilson

The Verification of Science and History

The Bible is continually verified by archaeology as new discoveries are made over the ages. Those who would deny the authenticity of the Bible are often silenced by new information that becomes available. For instance, until the mid-nineteenth century, the Babylonian king Belshazzar, mentioned in the record of the prophet Daniel, was unknown to secular history. All secular historical discoveries indicated that a king named Nabonidus, who is not mentioned in the Bible, was the last ruler of Babylon before it was conquered in 538 B.C. by Cyrus of Persia. This fact was a common complaint of those who rejected the Bible's accuracy. It wasn't until 2,400 years after these events, in 1854, that a tablet belonging to Nabonidus was unearthed that mentioned his son, Belshazzar. Following this discovery, critics still denied that Belshazzar had ever been king, since the kingdom was conquered during Nabonidus' reign. Moreover, much was made of the statement in Daniel 5 that Belshazzar made Daniel "third ruler" of the kingdom. This seemed odd, since no "second" ruler was known, and again, Nabonidus was king when Babylon fell. So this whole account was considered fabricated by those who had not come to trust the Bible.

Over time though, more artifacts were discovered that contained Nabonidus' banking records, among other things, and the picture became clear. As it turns out, Nabonidus was fond of travel. He was absent from the capital for long periods of time, and in his absence, his son Belshazzar was the regent king, with full authority. So not only was Belshazzar a real king of Babylon, but since he and his father were both rulers, it was perfectly understandable why Daniel was made "third" ruler.[14]

In another example, the Bible records that there was a powerful nation called the Hittites dominating the Middle East from about 1750 to about 1200 B.C. (and recent evidence suggests they were still around much later). This nation is mentioned throughout the earlier parts of the Old Testament. Again, until the late nineteenth century, secular history had no record of this people, and Bible critics in lock step with religious liberals considered these stories pure fantasy.

But around the turn of the century, an archaeological dig in Turkey began to uncover a previously unknown city. There archeologists discovered an extensive library with thousands of tablets written in a primitive Indo-European language. This ultimately was shown to be the capital city of the Hittite people and much was learned verifying the Bible account.

Again and again we see modern man, in his arrogance, thinking that this discovery or that one shows that the Bible cannot be trusted.[15] A recent example is that of the Biblical record of King Solomon's mines. There has never been an archeological find that verifies this story, and secular archeologists rightly feel that such a great store of riches would have left some evidence of its existence. This has been a point of contention between Biblical liberals and so-called literalists

---

[14] Interestingly, this relationship must have lasted for at most a few hours, since the Bible records that on that very night the armies of Cyrus invaded the capital and subdued Babylon (exactly as prophesied by Isaiah about 150 years earlier, by the way), setting up a governor named Darius in Belshazzar's place.

[15] One example is the so-called "problem" of starlight and time. Though there have been some excellent theories advanced, we do not at this time understand with any certainty how we could see light from stars billions of "light-years" away if the universe is only several thousand years old. Perhaps one day we will, but whether we ever do or not doesn't change the truth of the creation account any more than secular archeological history's lack of understanding of King Belshazzar invalidated that truth. This is an example of reasonable faith in what God has said.

for centuries. But in 2008, archeologists working in Jordan very likely verified a site previously eliminated as a possibility for the location of Solomon's mines.[16] Those who accept the Bible as God's record of history had no doubt that these mines existed. It was only those who elevate man's opinion and research above the Bible who doubted.

Again and again over time, new discoveries have shown that man's beliefs were in error. The ancient Biblical cities of Arad, Bethel, Capernaum, Dan, Ephesus, Gaza, Hezor, Hezbon, Jericho and Ninevah were all unknown to secular history for long periods of time until some modern archeological dig "discovered" them. The pool at Bethesda, for instance, mentioned only in John chapter five, was believed a fabrication until a site fitting the exact Biblical description—five covered colonnades and all—was unearthed in the nineteenth century. Archaeology and historical research have uncovered verification of numerous sites, personalities,[17] structures and even nations mentioned in the Bible that were previously unknown outside of its pages. Other scientific disciplines regularly turn up new discoveries that shed light on the truth of God's word. Time and time again throughout modern history, we have found new evidence that the Bible is true. But have we learned the lessons of history? As is so often true, many have not. As a Christian, though, it is exciting to realize how much is known beyond dispute about the accuracy of this astounding book. Surely this fact is depressing and confusing to those whose world view requires its refutation.

---

[16] D. Vergano, "Copper Mine in Jordan Could Be King Solomon's," *USA Today*, October 27, 2008.

[17] Until 1961, no evidence existed confirming that there was ever a Roman governor named Pontius Pilate. Many people of that generation and previous ones were told that he was a Biblical myth.

The Verification of Prophecy

The Bible's authority, though, does not stand on the accuracy of its history alone. Much time has been spent in the preceding chapters of this book establishing the reasonableness of believing in a reality beyond our physical senses. The Bible is a spiritual book as well as a historical one. It declares and expounds on this supernatural world that we have all sensed in ourselves. One way in which the Bible reveals the influence of supernatural inspiration is through prophecy. There are many who believe, in accordance with their world view, that any prophecy or prediction that comes true would have to be a matter of either luck or deception. In these people's minds, what circumstances would have the power to change their commitment to this belief? What if one person made, say, fifty different predictions that all came true and this person never made an incorrect one, would that do it? Or what if ten people from different countries and different generations each predicted the same event, and that event happened just as they predicted?

If that wouldn't be enough, then how about nearly three hundred prophecies made by several different men in different countries and different historical periods, most of whom had no knowledge of each other, about a man who would live hundreds of years after the last of them died? Would that finally be enough?

This is exactly what the Bible record shows. These prophecies were made about the man Jesus who would be God in human form and would reconcile mankind to the Creator from whom it was estranged. These prophecies, made hundreds and even thousands of years before Jesus was born, named the town of His birth and predicted details of His death, such as the piercing of His side and the casting of lots for His robe at the foot of the cross. They foretold that He would be a man of sorrow and suffering, that He would be immediately preceded in history by a man living in the desert who would declare His coming to those all around,[18] that He would be a direct descendent of King David and many other specific, detailed prophecies that were all fulfilled in this man. These predictions were so precise and so accurately borne out that skeptics long believed they must have been written after Jesus' lifetime on earth.

But again, the God of the universe saw to it that verification of the truth was somewhere for us to find, and sure enough, that compelling curiosity peculiar to *Homo sapiens* eventually led us to the Dead Sea, where an ancient copy of the book of Isaiah (containing a number of the prophecies about Jesus), along with many other texts, was found. These were dated between 120 and 100 B.C., removing all doubt that they pre-dated Christ's human life.

Did this change any minds? Perhaps some, but most skeptics have simply reverted to attributing such prophecies to various types of fraud or forcing improbable interpretations of them. How clearly true Jesus' words in Luke 24:25[19] seem in light of this. I often read and hear of demands by atheists that God reveal Himself more plainly to humankind. How much more overwhelmingly clear could He be?

The prophetic and historical accuracies of the Bible often join together in amazing, faith-building accounts.

But the prophecies about Jesus are not the only predictions made in the Bible. Not at all. The prophetic and historical accuracies of the Bible often join together in amazing, faith-

---

[18] Fulfilled in John the Baptist.
[19] *"He said to them, 'How foolish you are, and how slow of heart to believe all that the prophets have spoken!'"*

building accounts. One example is found in Ezekiel 26 and the history of the city of Tyre.

Modern Tyre (Sur) is a city of under 150,000 people on the southern coast of Lebanon. It's a city of rich history and many legends. Around 585 B.C., the prophet Ezekiel predicted that King Nebuchadnezzar of Babylon (Belshazzar's grandfather) would destroy Tyre. Originally, Tyre was a divided city, partly on the Mediterranean coast and partly on a small island off the coast, separated by a shallow channel. Ezekiel said that Tyre would be utterly destroyed, that many nations would fight against her, that the debris of the city would be thrown into the ocean, that the city would never be found again and that fishermen would come there to cast their nets.[20]

Well, the city of Tyre still exists, so this is another point of contention among those who have no interest in pursuing the whole story.

In 573 B.C., Nebuchadnezzar's armies, after years of siege, did destroy utterly the mainland city. However, many of the inhabitants escaped by boat to the island, and Nebuchadnezzar, as the prophecy also predicted, did not pursue them there. The city of Tyre remained a significant city just off the coast for more than two centuries, so most of the prophecy was not yet fulfilled. This must have been fodder for 240 years of criticism of Ezekiel's prophecies.

However, in 333 B.C., the eyes of Alexander the Great fell on Tyre, now a fortified island city. Using the 240-year-old debris of the razed mainland city, Alexander had a causeway built to the island (so the debris of the city was thrown into the ocean as predicted), and he completely destroyed the island city. Although Tyre was to be rebuilt on the coast and did reclaim some of its former importance, the site of the razed island city

---

[20] Ezekiel chapter 26.

was for long centuries a small fishing village where fishermen cast their nets. As Ezekiel promised, the entire *ancient* city lies in ruins, its debris cast into the sea.[21] Today, Alexander's causeway has filled in completely, creating a much different peninsula-city named, in the local language, Sur. So, the city of Tyre about which Ezekiel prophesied—the ancient city known to the world at that time—no longer exists, replaced by a much different city, with even a different name.

Ezekiel made no mistake in his prediction because he was not speaking out of his own mind and his own imagination. He was clearly doing something beyond the human, physical capability of men. He was inspired to make these predictions by an Entity that was trying to communicate with us, to verify His existence and His power. This story has many messages, but primarily that God's word is true and that what God has said can be trusted even when we haven't yet seen it fulfilled or when we don't fully understand it.

> *There is powerful evidence that the Bible can be trusted after all.*

The people who lived between 573 and 333 B.C. had a choice. They didn't have full verification of this prophecy as we do, so they could choose either to believe God or to believe themselves proper judges of God's word. Because of man's stubborn vanity and arrogance, there is no doubt that many scoffed and denied the truth of the prophecy. But some believed just *because they already had enough information to know* that God doesn't lie. This is what Jesus meant when He said, "Blessed are those who have not seen, and yet have believed."[22] We call it reasoned faith.

---

[21] The city was attacked often by Egypt, taken over by the Greek general Antigonus and dominated by the Seleucids. It eventually became a Roman province.

[22] John 20:29.

What about Other Religious Texts?

So, maybe there is powerful evidence that the Bible can be trusted after all. But atheists and agnostics often ask, "Why are these many other religious books to be rejected? What makes Christians think that they have the only revelation? Does every other religious writing have to be wrong?"

In a word, yes. The reason Christians reject the writings of other religions is partly because none compare by the farthest stretch of reason to the Bible in their historical, scientific and prophetic accuracy.[23] None were written by so many diverse authors or over such a span of time, maintaining unity and consistency of message. But the most important reason to reject the manuscripts of other religions is one that follows from the basic rules of logic (the "first principals" discussed in chapter one) and the facts detailed in this chapter. Because we have good reason to believe that the Bible is the inspired word of God, mutual exclusion demands that those teachings which conflict with the Bible be eliminated from consideration. Whether it's the Qur'an or *Science and Health with Key to the Scriptures*, the Kojiki (Shinto) or the Adi Sri Guru Granth Sahib (Sikh), all contain contradictions to what the most powerfully believable religious book has said. So they are logically not to be trusted.

Moreover, the Bible makes many exclusive claims to truth about God, not the least of which is Jesus' claim to be the only way to a relationship with Him. This is discussed further in chapter seven.

---

[23] Those written most recently, such as the Book of Mormon and others, may have some historical accuracy in recounting some more-modern events, but they don't have the accurate prophetic content of the Bible, and their veracity depends upon the word of one man alone.

Donald R. Wilson

The Apocrypha

Finally, many argue that we can't know what parts of the Bible may or may not be true because Christians can't even decide which writings should properly be included in it. Some say that many writings were suppressed by powerful political forces whose agenda was to gain control of this new religion along the way. We occasionally hear of discoveries of "lost gospels" that tell very different stories about Jesus. These almost immediately inspire books and articles (and sometimes movies) claiming or implying that this "new information" invalidates the Bible's claims. Whenever someone digs up some old papyrus fragment that appears to have some kind of religious content, it's immediately proof that the modern Bible is not complete, at best. Those who wish to discredit Christianity ask, "Why are these writings not included?"

These claims refer either to the apocrypha,[24] which is a group texts that have been left out of one canon (collection of writings accepted as inspired) or another, or to extra-Biblical writings of various sects or splinter groups. It's true that the Christian faith has struggled now and then over the centuries to come to a definitive conclusion as to exactly which books should be included in the Christian Bible. But these struggles arose from a proper interest in ensuring that the scripture remained pure and unsoiled by error. Therefore, all writings that came along from time to time were looked at carefully by church leaders for internal and external affirmation that they were consistent with those writings that were known to be genuine. This would be a normal and expected process in the early life of a new movement such as this.

---

[24] The Apocrypha (capitalized) refers to thirteen to seventeen Old Testament books included by early Greek and Latin translators and accepted by the Catholic and Eastern Orthodox churches but not included in the Protestant scriptures. Uncapitalized, it refers generally to all writings not included in either the Old or New Testament of a given canon.

A thorough discussion of the various complaints about how the Bible reached its current form is beyond the scope of this book, but it is an interesting study and one that any seeker of truth should undertake. It's enough for our purposes here to say the following.

Regarding the Old Testament; the material included in the Protestant Bible was established by ancient Judaism long before the Christian faith was born. For many reasons, Protestants have generally decided that these long trusted historical documents are the only ones that can be confidently understood as inspired, God-breathed scripture. Meanwhile, various Catholic traditions accept certain material that was written after about 400 B.C. and before the birth of Jesus.[25] At one point, these writings were integrated into the Hebrew Scriptures by certain Jewish leaders when translating assorted available writings from Hebrew to Greek. This same material was then accepted by some early Christian leaders when creating a major Latin translation called the Vulgate. Many Apocryphal books contain beautiful or poetic stories that can be effective in making points or teaching character and therefore have their uses. Most have more of the flavor of a secular history of the Jews during the time in which they were written. I am not an expert on the contents of the Apocryphal writings, but I know of only one notable doctrine of contention between Catholicism and Protestantism arising from these writings. So, this additional material contains little important doctrine that conflicts with the traditional Hebrew Scriptures.

> *The material included in the Protestant Bible was established by ancient Judaism.*

---

[25] The writings of this period were rejected by the Jews primarily because God had not provided a prophet to lead the Jewish people during this time, and hence, there was no authoritative teaching being handed down by God during this period.

Regarding the New Testament, there were a great number of writings about Jesus, the apostles, and the Christian faith in general in the first few centuries following the amazing period of history known as the life of Christ. There were many agendas behind these writings, some pure, some misguided and some evil. Quite a number of them are obvious attempts to make credible certain derivative belief systems that arose over the centuries (most notably Gnosticism). Some of the apocryphal works from the first few centuries were wonderful writings that were very much loved by the early churches. The historical record shows much discussion about the different works among the elders who led the church after the passing of the eyewitnesses. Some documents were exposed clearly as spurious, but some were frankly difficult to be sure about. In the end, church leaders wisely decided to include only those writings verifiably produced by bona fide eyewitnesses or those who were close to and personally acquainted with Jesus' eyewitness followers. These are the 27 books included today in virtually all New Testaments.

Much could be said about this, but it is a distraction from the core issue—that of the authority of God's word. If there is a canon used by a truly Christian denomination somewhere that includes writings contradictory to the rest of scripture or unsupportable by thorough scholarship, then that denomination is wrong to be including it. It is not a part of the Bible if it conflicts with it. If a book is included in some canon and it is historically and spiritually accurate and useful for correct moral or historical teaching when compared to the rest of scripture, then it does no real harm, whether truly inspired or not.

The Bible is a complex document written by ancient peoples of varying cultures. It makes complicated truth claims about history and the nature of reality that are not pleasing to the ear of modern, egotistical mankind (including such self-described "brights" as the new atheists). If a person wishes to discredit the

Bible, as so many do, he or she only needs to engage in a superficial and slanted study of it and of its history. Professing themselves to be wise in the process, such scholars become fools,[26] tripped up by their own wishful thinking and shallow research. Because of the philosophical bias with which they approach the study, they will always stop short of reaching a full understanding of what they are reading. When dramatic claims are made based on "new evidence" or "long-suppressed information," be careful to know the whole story before you buy into it.

The Implications of the Bible's Teachings

A seeker who lays aside bias and truly seeks to understand will see that in the Bible we have an historical account that, to the mind of any scientist, historian or layman open to the possibility of its truth, plausibly explains the early history of the world, the origin of languages, the source of races and cultures and the rise of the many different religions of the world. It explains cave men, dinosaurs, and plate tectonics, among many other

The Bible maintains a striking consistency of theme and message.

modern "dilemmas," if one just cares to look with the mind of an honest seeker. Given the time span, as well as the number of diverse authors and their geographical dispersion, the only expected outcome would be chaos, yet the Bible maintains a striking consistency of theme and message, and in my view, a complete lack of contradiction. Hundreds of prophecies were made and fulfilled, and archaeology continues to confirm the Bible's every claim.

---

[26] Wording taken from Romans 1:22.

Any sincere person is compelled to ask himself the implications of this. Can such a comprehensive and detailed collection of ancient manuscripts with this level of apparent reliability be ignored? Does it comport with any sense of reason to declare such a document irrelevant to our lives?

As Martin Luther implied in his quote opening this chapter, Christianity is inexorably rooted in the authority of the word of God. If the Bible is not fully true as written according to the plain meaning of the language and context, from the first verse to the last, then there is no reason to accept Christ as anything but another lunatic leader on par with Jim Jones and David Koresh.

How Do We Know We Understand What the Bible Really Means to Say?

We humans, in our consistent way, have over time seriously confused and distorted the scriptures in perhaps every way possible. This comes about from various motives that have existed throughout history. It is of course true that because the Bible is ancient, it is written in a way that is, in places, confusing to the modern ear. But there is no reason that most of the Bible, and certainly its essential principles, can't be understood by any person reading it if one simply puts aside agenda and uses the same principles in understanding it that one would use in reading any original work of history or philosophy.

There are a number of literary styles used in the Bible, as one might expect from the diverse sources and circumstances from which it came. There is plenty of metaphor, a device Jesus loved to use to bring life to His teachings: "I am the vine and ye are the branches," for instance. Metaphor is also used extensively in prophetic passages. You will find poetic language, hyperbole, symbolism and perhaps most every literary device known, if you want to catalogue them. But the point is, you will know them when you see them unless you have an interest in making them something they are not.

A great deal of the Bible is also made up of narrative historical accounts. In fact, this style accounts for the vast majority of the Bible. Sections that record events and say, "this happened, and then this happened" are almost always narrative and should be taken as the inspired account of what actually occurred. There is no more reason to force these accounts to be metaphorical or poetic than there is for doing the same to a modern narrative.

In many passages, context is important. Some things were said to specific people for their specific time and circumstance. They may teach us principles that are useful in our culture and time, but common sense dictates that they are not to be emulated literally.

This is neither a liberal nor a stiffly literal approach to the scripture, but a common sense, contextual one. The Bible should be approached with an open, seeking mind free of personal agenda and read in a natural way. It is often important to have an understanding of the cultural and political backdrop as well. With this approach, people of every age and academic ability can glean rich wisdom and understanding from it.

Chapter Six

Why Does God Seem So Angry and Sometimes Even Cruel?

"The Christian god is a three headed monster; cruel, vengeful and capricious. If one wishes to know more of this raging, three headed beast-like god, one only needs to look at the caliber of the people who say they serve him."

—Thomas Jefferson

In discussing why the God of the Bible should be understood as the one true God, it is important to consider one of the most-often voiced objections to accepting and honoring Him, if He does exist. To most people now and then, God does seem something like a "three-headed monster." It's unclear what may have evoked such hostility from Jefferson, but a cooler head might have said that the history of God's interaction with man does, from time to time, raise a question in the mind of an honest observer as to whether or not God's choices and actions were fair, given the situation.

The Wrath of God

There are many accounts in scripture that, at first glance, give the impression that God is capricious at best. There were times when God ordered His people to wipe out whole people groups and sent instant death by various means in response to seemingly minor offenses. Yet, He has sometimes overlooked and evidently condoned behavior that is appalling to modern moral sensitivities. Once, He even destroyed all of mankind except for a very small remnant. Could these be the acts of a loving Creator whose whole purpose in creating the universe was to commune with and love a creature something like himself? Many see accounts such as that of the great flood as the acts of an arbitrary, vindictive God. After all, could *everyone* living at that time, including young children, have deserved summary execution except for the righteous eight? Was there no one at all among men aside from Noah who was making an honest effort to follow and honor God as best he understood Him? The God of the past, as presented in the Bible, is sometimes hard to see as loving, and this is a sentiment fervently seized upon by the assertive atheists of our time.

For many, the God of the present is not much better. It's easy to doubt the love of God when we see cruelty, hunger, poverty and suffering in our world. Because of the influence of naturalism, most people seem to have a hazy acceptance of death as a necessary thing (though they work hard at never thinking about it), but they wonder why God allows the agonizing and premature death of the innocent. If He is indeed all-knowing, why would He allow the horrible 9/11/2001 attacks to go forward and all those innocent people to be killed? If God is just, why is evil not *always* punished evenhandedly? And why are we all not equally blessed and happy?

And what of the God of the future? How could a loving God send people to a place like hell, with such cruel and final judgment?

On this very compelling subject of God's choices, it's difficult to know where to start in order to end up with a well-ordered discussion. There are so many concepts at issue here. Generally, though, if one is to understand God's dealings with man, he has to begin by understanding

- who God is,
- who man is compared to God,
- what the relationship between the two was meant to be, and
- what it has become.

Only then will a person begin to understand why God does what He does and allows what He allows.

Just like those who question the existence of any god, those whose sensibilities are offended by the accounts of God's wrath or His apparent apathy toward pain and evil are not digging deep enough to get an understanding of the whole picture. It's that same problem of not understanding things as they truly are; that *world view* thing is in the way again. In order to feel this way about God, one has to be working from the presupposition that God is a being mostly like oneself—that He knows the same facts and interprets them the same way, that He is subject to the same feelings, the same limitations and the same laws and perhaps most importantly, that He has the same agenda.

Who We're Dealing With

If a person seeks to understand God, he must start by viewing Him as The Creator. Those who say, "How could a loving God...?" or "God should..." are operating from the idea that their understanding and judgment somehow approach equality with God's and that they are therefore qualified to make judgments about His choices. This idea has to be quashed if we are to understand at all. Surely, if a Being is self-existent and powerful enough to speak into existence matter from nothing and put in place complex laws that have taken mankind centuries to only partially understand, and if this Being put time itself in place and has authority over all that He has made, then He is not much like us in most ways. Yes, He has said that we were created to resemble Him (in His image), but obviously that does not mean anything approaching equality with Him in knowledge, power or understanding.

If you think about it, God has instilled in us the idea of *"perfect"* based on Himself. I pointed out in a previous chapter that God is perfect by definition. We didn't invent the definition of perfect out of our imaginations. When we describe something as perfect, we are saying that it is without flaw. But why do we view one thing as flawed, and another as flawless? This measuring stick, along with the moral yardstick that we've discussed, has been placed in our psyche by our Creator out of His mind and His perspective. If we are honest, we understand internally that we are not flawless beings. Only the most deluded narcissist would disagree. But if we know this, then it follows logically that we know what

> *God has instilled in us the idea of "perfect" based on Himself.*

we are comparing ourselves to when we make this judgment. We know that we are imperfect and limited copies of some perfect being. Otherwise, there would be no basis for us to say that we are imperfect. If that Being is the Creator God, and He did, in fact, create all that we see, then He is the standard by which everything in our experience would naturally be judged. What other being would be a candidate for this comparison?

Atheist biologist Richard Dawkins has dubbed this idea the "argument from degree," questioning whether or not there has to be something perfect for comparison just because we see that we are not perfect. He quite hilariously analogizes that if some people stink, there must be a "perfectly peerless stinker" to which we are comparing them.[1] One has to laugh when he reads this, but it is also immediately obvious that this is a "red herring" type of argument. It leads us on an intellectual wild goose chase, ignoring the fact that the question here is the concept of perfection itself, not some subjective judgment of an environmental stimulus. The two don't compare at all. One exists in our minds' eye on an endless scale of variability, while the other is an objective standard by which we judge ourselves. And that's exactly the point.

Judging God

If God is our standard of perfection, and we know that we don't reach that standard, is it reasonable and proper for us to construct our own standard by which to judge Him? On what basis would we be justified in doing so? This would be placing the created above the Creator, which violates the requirement of logic that the Creator must be greater than His creation. It would be the same as pouring ourselves a cup of coffee and judging it to be one pint, then criticizing a pint container because it doesn't hold the whole amount when we pour our cup of coffee into it. That would be placing our judgment above an absolute standard. So when we reason it out fully, we see that *it is simply not within our range of insight and understanding to make value judgments about the acts of a Creator so much greater than ourselves.* Because He is who He is, His actions are correct on their face.

Moreover, declaring moral judgments against God's acts is a completely self-defeating argument for the unbeliever. First, it presupposes that there is a God in order to build a platform for not believing in Him. Why say that you choose not to believe in

---

[1] R. Dawkins, *The God Delusion* (New York: Bantam Press, 2006).

a God who would or would not do this or that? If He does this or that, then He exists, so using that reason to say you don't believe He exists is chaotic thinking. Second, I said in chapter two that the only possible source of *objective* moral values is a morally perfect Being. If we attempt to judge God's acts by a moral standard that we think should apply to everyone, including Him, then we admit that such an objective standard exists and therefore that God, the standard giver, must indeed exist in accordance with the moral argument. In short, unbelievers invalidate their own belief system on many counts when they rail against the choices of an almighty God.

Not So Bad After All

Though we have no justified basis for railing against God, we were not created ignorant. We were given the gift of judgment similar to (though nowhere near equal to) that of our Creator, and we are expected to use it. If we dig deeply, presupposing on good grounds that what God did was right, we will usually find that these accounts of Biblical history which give the impression that God is cruel or disinterested become less offensive when we understand them more fully. An honest seeker who diligently studies these episodes will find again and again that God had usually withheld his righteous judgment over many years from a given people, allowing multiple opportunities for them to turn from their evil actions or intentions before exhausting his patience. At other times, a deeper look makes it obvious that God had no acceptable choice but to severely and instantly mete out punishment for offenses that may seem small at first glance but that were, in

> *Unbelievers invalidate their own belief system on many counts when they rail against the choices of an almighty God.*

fact, important breaches of righteous conduct or immediate threats to God's just plans and needed to be dealt with decisively. In other words, if we truly seek to understand, we will come closer to agreeing with the judgments made by the Creator, after whose judgment our own has been patterned.

One example is the way in which God dealt with a people group called the Amalekites. In I Samuel 15:3, God told Saul, Israel's new king, to *"go, attack the Amalekites and totally destroy everything that belongs to them. Do not spare them; put to death men and women, children and infants, cattle and sheep, camels and donkeys."* Saul mostly complied, but on the surface the account implies that he tried to show a modicum of mercy by saving the Amalekite king. A brief first reading also indicates that Saul tried to be generous to his soldiers by allowing them to loot some of the best goods, a common practice and one that the soldiers would have expected as part of their pay.

But when Samuel, God's prophet at the time, found out about Saul's handling of the situation, he required that Saul bring the Amalekite king before him. Then, in front of Saul, Samuel was led to hack the captured king to death with his sword. Samuel then prophesied that God would remove Saul from the throne.

Wow! If ever there was an example of a vindictive, hateful God, this would have to be it. Kill children and infants? Destroy even their animals? Hack their king to pieces? Punish Saul for trying to show mercy? How could God be any more impulsive and cruel? Is it possible Thomas Jefferson might have just finished reading this passage when he made the dramatic statement at the head of this chapter? I can imagine the

> *The most critical thing in understanding God is to internalize the fact that He is God and we are not.*

rant of some of our current atheist writers when they come across this account. And of course there are others like it. This account is similar to the case of the Midianites recorded in Numbers chapter 31, for instance, where God required His people to kill everyone in Midian, women and children included, leaving only the virgins alive.

First of all, even if commands such as these were given by God and the results were recorded in the Bible without any context or explanation, it would still be reasonable for us to ask, "What business is it of mine?" To reiterate the previous point, *the most critical thing in understanding God is to internalize the fact that He is God and we are not. Imagining that this relationship were different is the root of all human evil.*

The Creator Owns His Creation

We have said that God is our measure of perfection, but this account shades His position a little differently. If God is indeed the author of all life, then He is, by right, the owner of it. This is another logical attribute of a Being who is truly the Creator. What has been made belongs to its maker. It is God's right to extinguish the life that He alone has ignited. It belongs to Him, to do with as He pleases. This fact certainly is not comforting to human sensibilities, but God exists in a plane above human sensibilities. He has plans we do not know about. He sees what we don't see. I was once told by an employer to remember that I only had the "lower left corner" of the big picture in the operation of the company. Well, when it comes to the flow of human history into the future in accordance with God's plans, we don't even have the lower left square micron of His big picture! When we question His actions, we are questioning the One who came up with the laws of relativity, motion, gravity, electricity, hydraulics, pneumatics, thermodynamics and countless other complex, intricate, interdependent laws in a flash of brilliance beyond our imagination by simply saying, *"Let there be…"*

Even if we never understand a particular choice God has made, the most we can say is simply *that*—that we don't understand. To assume that we can pass judgment on such a being as God is ludicrous. Speaking for the Creator God, the prophet Isaiah said,

> *"For My thoughts are not your thoughts, nor are your ways My ways," says the Lord. For as the heavens are higher than the earth, so are My ways higher than your ways, and My thoughts than your thoughts."* [2]

When you consider the power and knowledge necessary to do what God has done, this is certainly an understatement.

To us, as beings bound to a physical existence, death is the ultimate bad news, the most severe possible penalty. But we forget that, because of our willful rebellion, God will eventually take back every physical life that He has given. In the end, we will all have to suffer the just penalty for our sin.[3] It's just a matter of timing. The point here is that we simply refuse to believe and trust that such a being as God would, by His nature, always know perfectly what is best for His perfect purposes. We value our physical lives above His purposes and place our own judgment above His. We dare to think we should be the ones to decide what is fair and just, rejecting the Author of fairness and justice. This is rebellion against righteousness (another word for

---

[2] Isaiah 55:8,9.

[3] Because God's love and mercy are equal to His justice, physical, permanent death (loss of existence) is not the final result of sin unless we choose that for ourselves. Barring Christ's return, death will certainly extinguish our physical life one day, but thanks to His work at the cross, death does not have to be the ultimate victor over our eternal self, as described in chapter two.

perfection). The Creator God is the definition of righteousness, and such rebellion is the definition of sin.

So if we truly understand our place in this relationship, we know, even without context, that for some reason the Amalekite nation was worthy only of genocide. We know this because we know that the judgment was made by the only proper Authority for making such a judgment.

There Is Always a Reason

In this case, though, as is true most of the time in scripture, God has not shared his actions with us and left us to shrug our shoulders as to His motives and justifications. He does not need to justify Himself to us because, again, He personifies justice. But neither does he want us to believe that He does things without cause. Those who make a thorough and honest attempt to know God by studying *all* of His word and who don't suffer from the bias and intellectual laziness of our current vocal atheists usually come to realize that the God of the Bible is never capricious.

As recorded in the book of Genesis, God had made a covenant with Abraham, the father of the Israelite nation. He said, "*I will bless those who bless you, and whoever curses you I will curse.*"[4] This was a promise not just to Abraham but to the nation he was to father. It turns out that it was the stated purpose of the Amalekites, their manifesto, if you will, that they would destroy the Israelites completely.[5] They had already tried. During the exodus from Egypt, Amelek had ruthlessly attacked the Israelites from the rear, slaughtering women and children in an attempt to destroy the nation by attacking their weakest point. They were a violent, marauding people, and

---

[4] Genesis 12:3.
[5] Let's hope for their sakes that the people groups of our modern world who hate Israel will not suffer a similar fate.

they showed no mercy.[6] God's people had been attacked and harassed by them many times and God had vowed to *"completely blot out the memory of Amalek from under heaven."*[7] God knew the level of their hate and the degree of their determination and capability, both present and future. It is likely that the Amalekites, had any lived, would have pursued Israel to the last man. We don't know His full reasoning for sure, but God was there, seeing not just the present but also motives and plans and future events—the big picture.

Aside from protecting His chosen people, God may have had other just reasons for what He did to the Amalekites. For one thing, this is certainly an object lesson to those who would rise up against the God of Creation. He is a fearful and terrible opponent, and a powerful ally.

Another appropriate question that arises from this account is, "What about Saul?" God had only recently chosen him to rule over the nation, and then he was informed that he would be removed from the throne. Did God make an error in judgment in choosing Saul, or did this event cause Him to change His mind?

Saul was appointed for God's reasons. The account in I Samuel reveals that the people had demanded a king, and God appointed one because although He knew they didn't need one, their desire was within what many scholars call God's permissible will. But God had already planned to give them a proper leader, a man after His own heart, named David. In the meantime, out of love for them, He gave Israel a tall, handsome king, leader-like in the human sense, to placate their desires. God knew Saul would fail, that he would try to hide his disobedience and that he would value his position above his

---

[6] Deuteronomy 25:17-19.
[7] Recorded in the reference above and in Exodus 17:14.

relationship with the One who placed him there. As always, God could see what man couldn't, that Saul's motive in disobeying was not to show mercy to the Amalekite king or to show generosity to his troops but to elevate himself before his people. Saul spared the enemy king in order to parade him before the Israelites in a show of pride, and he allowed the soldiers to pillage in order to gain their favor. Then he looked into the eyes of God's prophet and lied about his motives. Saul valued being important and popular with his subjects more than he valued obedience to his own Master.

Before time, God knew the exact day in which Saul would be replaced. Saul was actually allowed to reign for over forty years after this day, but God knew that Saul's descendents could not be allowed to succeed him because God had always had other plans. In this account, He was just informing Saul ahead of time. No, as Samuel made clear in this passage, *"God is not a man, that He should change His mind."*[8]

God's Unmerited Mercy

It's easy for any person not interested in recognizing God's proper authority or for a person who is hurt, bitter or angry to see God as an ogre. But it's clear from the Biblical accounts that God is interested in establishing a relationship with us and keeping it on track as He intended it to be. There have been billions who, like the Amalekites, have tried to interfere, and all who have done so[9] have risked a collision with God's justice. Many have suffered just consequences, but vastly more have escaped, by God's mercy, to try again. "The amazing thing may not be so much that some [have been] impacted by God's wrath as that anyone has ever been a beneficiary of His mercy. His

---

[8] The idea to use the Amalekite example was inspired by a sermon by Mr. Justin Nalls, a youth minister in Birmingham, Alabama, in April 2008.
[9] All of us.

mercy is undeserved. He proceeds to judgment with reluctance (Ezekiel 18:23). Yet in the end, not because He is cruel but because He is holy, He will judge evil."[10]

I established in chapter two that God is a personal entity. It takes a personality to make choices and act upon them. The Bible describes God as an entity with a personality much like ours. He has emotions, He grieves and He hates. Because He is complete in Himself, he has no needs, but clearly He wants and He loves, just as we do.

> *If God were never angry, evil would have free reign in our world.*

Ask yourself how you would feel if, after laboring for days to "create" something—something of the highest possible importance and value to you—someone willfully damaged, distorted or tried to completely destroy it. Is it not reasonable for the emotion of anger to well up in you in such a case? God is rightly outraged when His work is damaged or distorted, especially when it is done willfully.

Further, if God were never angry, evil would have free reign in our world. If He were indifferent to the attacks of men upon His people and His plans, things would never be set right, and we would be complaining about that instead![11] In fact, many in our age are making that exact complaint.

Is God Apathetic?

But the actions of God are not the only attributes questioned

---

[10] *AIIA Institute Proclamation*, Vol. 18, No. 1, January-February 2008. Author is unknown. Ezekiel 18:23 reads: "'Do I take any pleasure in the death of the wicked?' declares the Sovereign Lord. 'Rather, am I not pleased when they turn from their ways and live?'"

[11] Thanks to my friend, Rev. Fred A. Johns for sharing the preceding two points in a sermon.

by secularists of all stripes, and often by believers as well. We also tend to be concerned about His inaction. If he loves us, why does He not fix things for us? How can He allow the horrors that we see around our world every day? Is He weak, or just apathetic? Sadly, this subject comes up often in our fallen world, and these questions are asked sincerely by so many that it has been the subject of many articles, books, lessons, homilies and sermons throughout our history. The majority of adults have found themselves, at some point in their lives, either asking these questions for themselves or groping for encouraging answers for someone else who desperately needs them. So, it's important to try to understand what is going on here.

I said that in order to understand God's actions, we first need to understand what the relationship between God and man was meant to be and what it has become. Evil exists because of the choices of free created beings. Genesis 3 records clearly that the first man and woman initiated the rift between the holy, perfect God and the humans He created for His pleasure. They were influenced by the character of Satan, a being that had been created in many ways similar to them, especially in the sense that he possessed free will, which he had used to choose rebellion against God. But Satan, unlike Adam and Eve, was a supernatural being with a great deal of understanding about how things really are that the first couple may not have had. The evil one, inhabiting a serpent's body, used a simple, powerful and deceitful form of logic to influence Eve to believe she had the wisdom to make her own decisions, regardless of what God had said. This is the first occurrence of the incredible arrogance that has infected all of Eve's descendents. She even bought into the ridiculous notion that she could judge God a liar. How sad that Adam came along, following so easily in Eve's error without even the need for Satan's trickery. Even sadder is the fact that we come along, as Adam's sons and daughters, and so easily do the same.

This is an incredibly powerful account with many lessons and implications for life as we live it today, but they are mostly beyond the scope of our purpose here. The essential point is that man chose, using the freedom of choice—the independence—granted to him by his Creator, to disobey. In this act of defiance, he effectively said to God, *I do not trust you to run my life. I do not believe you will always act in my best interests and maintain the perfect environment and existence that I have known thus far. I think I can do it better. I think I'm smarter and more capable than You are. Never mind that I'm completely aware that You spoke into existence everything that I see, including myself, in a mere six days. I still think I'm the proper one to be in charge of my life.* Since this defining moment in history, the heart of man has been *"deceitful above all things, and desperately wicked."* [12]

On this matter of original sin, people often protest with questions like, "Why do we all have to suffer the consequences of Adam's choice?" It's a good question. Why shouldn't we all have been born with a fresh opportunity to be obedient and enjoy God's blessing?

To get a handle on this, a person has to be sure he or she understands how things were before Adam and Eve's choices were made. It's hard for us to envision a perfect world where death, sorrow and suffering do not exist—where all the laws of nature work in perfect harmony with one another, sustained in this perfect condition by God for His own pleasure. Yet the Christian believes, by the revelation of scripture, that this is exactly how things were after God completed creation. When He was finished fashioning His universe, God pronounced His work, *"Very good."* [13] I've already established that God is the only reasonable example of *perfect*. If this is so, then wouldn't "very

---

[12] Jeremiah 17:9.
[13] Genesis 1:31.

good" to such a Being mean, for all intents and purposes, perfect? How could a perfect Being judge anything "very good" unless it was perfect? So it follows that Adam and Eve were beneficiaries of a perfect creation. So perfect, the Bible implies, that there weren't even thorns and thistles to interfere with man's enjoyment of it.

Death and suffering did not exist during this period of perfection created by God. The relationship between man and God was as God intended it to be. Man enjoyed all the blessings of creation freely. He communed with God and nature openly, and because he understood God's incredible power, wisdom and love, he submitted himself to Him, not out of fear but out of the knowledge that God was vastly better suited to run things than he. At that time, man understood fully who God was, who man was compared to God and what the relationship between them was meant to be. This short period of history is a snapshot of God's perfect will for our world. But man was free to choose how he would live. He was not compelled to love and serve God, because that kind of love and service is meaningless. Coerced servitude is not a real relationship in the mind of God (which is why, as His creation, it's not a real relationship in our minds either).

Obviously, free choice is a two-edged sword. That's why God allowed it. He wanted to be loved by a creation who could freely *choose* to love him. If anything is obvious from scripture, this is. God wanted to be vulnerable because love can't be given or received without exposing oneself to the possibility of rejection. If all possibility of rejection is removed, then it is at best benevolent despotism, not love. God is already the ruler and owner of all creation. He didn't need more subjects; He needed a people to love.

Donald R. Wilson

Who Is Responsible for Evil in the World?

William P. Young, in his fanciful novel, *The Shack*, created a character named Mack Phillips, who had a unique opportunity (to say the least) to have a weekend visit with God. In this story, Mack had been struggling to recover from the brutal murder of his beloved daughter and he had become bitterly disappointed with God. When asked how an all-powerful being could allow this, God (in the story, a folksy female personification of Him) personally explains the problem of evil in the world this way:

> *"No one knows what horrors I've saved the world from 'cuz people can't see what never happened. All evil flows from independence, and independence is your choice. If I were to simply revoke all the choices of independence, the world as you know it would cease to exist <u>and love would have no meaning</u>. This world is not a playground where I keep all my children free from evil. Evil is the chaos of this age that you brought to me, but it will not have the final say. Now it touches everyone that I love, those who follow me and those who don't. If I take away the consequences of people's choices, I destroy the possibility of love. Love that is forced is no love at all."* [14]

A man wants to run his own life, so he makes the independent choice to hate his neighbor or to cheat his business partner. A woman, in her desire for "the good life" that comes from independence, chooses to sleep with a married man or perhaps even to take a life in the selfish hope of making hers better. An insane, hate-engorged jihadist, as an exercise of his free will, plans and executes mass murder on foreign soil in a

---

[14] W. Young, *The Shack* (Newbury Park, CA: Windblown Media, 2007). Underlining added.

confused attempt to "do God's will." By his own insistence, man is free to make choices independent of God's guidance and direction. But those choices have consequences. When we receive the just consequences of our choices or someone else's, we rail at God for not saving us from them. In *The Shack*, God went on to say, *"You demand your independence, but then complain that I actually love you enough to give it to you."* [15]

God is not the author of evil and suffering in the world, man is. So if we understand evil properly, when we see it, as we do every day, we will not shake our fist at God but will shake our head and ask, "How could *we* have messed things up so badly?"

The Reason We Are Separated from God

In addition to being an all-powerful creator and a loving sustainer, God has another attribute. As I discussed briefly before, He is holy. The idea of holiness is one that is difficult for many to understand, partly because it is not a word we use in common speech and it seems reserved for church and religious discussions. Some might call it "Christianese" or "Religionese." This is because in its highest sense, it is a word reserved for God alone. But it is really an easy word because it is simply another near-synonym for moral perfection. God possesses a virtuousness that is beyond reproach, and as such, He cannot commune with moral error (called *sin* in the Bible). It's not that God, through his powerful will, maintains Himself in a state of holiness in spite of all the opportunities and temptations in His environment that might cause Him to err. That would be a description of us if we had God's power. Rather, holiness is God's *nature*. Because He is the definition of perfection, He is

> *God is not the author of evil and suffering in the world, man is.*

---

[15] Young, *The Shack*.

perfect by definition in all that He does. He can no more commune[16] with unholiness and error than we can maintain holiness in our own power. The two opposites cannot coexist.

So, when prodded by Satan's deception, the first couple exercised their free choice and rejected their Creator, they broke with the perfect nature created in them and entered a world apart from God; a world where moral error exists and where a holy God cannot go. The relationship was forever broken.

It can't be overemphasized that this is not what God intended. The apostle Paul made this clear when he said, *"Before the creation of the world, [God] chose us through Christ to be holy and perfect in his presence."*[17] Of course, God knew that this relationship would be corrupted, but it was not His will that it should.

God had created a holy relationship with mankind, which at that time consisted of only two people. That holiness was broken and soiled by willful disobedience by one man and one woman, yes, but through them, by all of mankind. A little honest thought will reveal that the idea of a new, unsoiled relationship with every offspring of Adam would have been untenable. All living things are born after their own kind (Genesis 1:24) and humankind has been corrupted through the sin of its progenitor, Adam. We are born into this corruption. Humans cannot live a holy life in the midst of unholiness, any more than a holy God can exist in it. That would require a coexistence between the two that is, as I've said, not possible. This is the whole reason why God could not continue to relate to Adam while he was still in his error. The relationship was with God's special creation, mankind, not with one man and one woman, and once broken by mankind, the deed was done for all.

---

[16] To commune: to converse together, or be together, with profound intensity, intimacy and mutual service (author's definition).
[17] Ephesians 1:4.

When man was still holy, the world was still perfect. Man's holiness was part of this perfection, *which was upheld by the power of God*. The Bible makes it clear that all of nature is sustained by God at all times.[18] If God were to withdraw his sustaining power from the universe, it would fall apart and cease to exist (see example at the end of this chapter). Even in a perfect world, man could not achieve perfection, or holiness, without God's active will holding him up, as it was in the Garden of Eden.

> *If God were to withdraw his sustaining power from the universe, it would fall apart and cease to exist.*

At the time of Adam's sin (known as *the fall*), God withdrew some of His sustaining power from nature, including man. Things began to wind down. The ground lost some of its rich nutrients, genetic information began copying imperfectly, entropy was given free reign, and nothing was ever quite perfect again. This was God's just punishment for Adam and Eve's act of arrogant willfulness. Obviously, considering oneself a proper judge of God is the gravest of sins. Not unforgivable, it's clear, but capable of separating us from our Creator completely and bringing His just punishment upon us.

The punishment was given once, and for all mankind. God no longer supplies man with the sustaining power he needs for maintaining a continuous holy relationship with Him. Because that power is not available, no man can do it. Because of the condition of the world into which we are born, we will fail morally, or sin. And it won't take long. So there is no sense wishing we could have our own personal chance at a perfect relationship with God. It is not a possibility.

---

[18] Colossians 1:17, Hebrews 1:3.

Donald R. Wilson

Why Such an Awful Place as Hell?

The idea of a place of eternal punishment is really a stumbling point for many who ponder the Christian belief system. It seems reasonable to ask how a loving God could even contemplate such a place, much less carry it through. As His creation, very few of us could bring ourselves to force someone into a flaming torture for eternity. So how could our Creator, whose patience, love and goodness far exceed our own, devise and implement such a punishment? The Bible gives many descriptions of a place of judgment that is so terrible that we can't even try to imagine it without cringing and blocking it out.

The doctrine of hell has been a difficult and divisive subject for theologians and laymen throughout church history. Church leaders have commonly used it to frighten the laity into claiming devotion to the faith and complying with every edict handed down to them. Even today, leaders of many diverse religious congregations, believing the end justifies the means, wield the fear of eternal suffering like a loaded gun, coercing the unsaved to enter the fold. It's often sort of a short cut to persuasion. The church has argued over whether to believe hell is an actual place or more of a destiny, who will have to go to hell, whether there will be any posthumous chances to avoid it and whether or not the frightening descriptions of hell in the Bible are to be understood as literal.

So, what should those who contemplate Christianity think of the doctrine of hell? Is it real, and what will it be like for those whose choice is to decline reconciliation with God?

The truth is, I don't know. It's my belief that in revealing and describing hell, God is limited by the humanness of those He inspired to write about it. The same is true about heaven, actually. It's very much like the descriptions of bizarre visions given to some of the prophets and to the apostle John about future events that they did not have the range of experience to understand. They did the best they could under the constraints of their language and culture to relate the message that they had been given, and we do our best to understand what God was telling us in these inspired accounts. The language used in describing the eternal suffering of hell (flames, darkness, gnashing of teeth, thirst, flesh-eating worms and so forth) may or may not be metaphorical when considered from the standpoint of common use of language. From reading the passages as one would read any literary work, one doesn't necessarily get a reliable sense of the intent. So it's open to interpretation, and this is what causes controversy.

For me, it doesn't matter. There is one thing that I do know about hell. *It is final separation from God.* Consider for a moment what this means.

Because God has told us so in His word, Christians believe that God is the Creator and Sustainer of everything good in this world.[19] But hell is the place (or perhaps the circumstance) where God is not. If we understand our reality correctly, we realize that there could be no worse situation. Can you imagine everything that you think of as good in any way being absent from your life? Not only absent, but never again available. Love, comfort, satisfaction, friendship, peace, joy, wonder, beauty, strength, achievement, rest and any other thing that one would call good would be absent. And perhaps worst of all would be the absence of hope.

> *Hell is the place...where God is not.*

Those who make the choice to live independently of the Author of everything good eventually get their way. They ultimately receive what they have been asking for all along—complete independence from God. Hell is not a construct of

---

[19] James 1:17.

an angry God—it is His final reluctant capitulation to the choices made by a free person. God knows the extent of the consequences of that horrible choice and has, in love, given many warnings about it and descriptions of what it will be like. He is obviously concerned and saddened that anyone would choose it. But God, by His own design and His nature, has no option in this matter. Either man has free will or he doesn't. In allowing the thing known as hell, God honors a person's final decision by backing out of his or her consciousness completely. "Hell is not a place where people are consigned because they were pretty good blokes, but they just didn't believe the right stuff. They're consigned there, first and foremost, because they defy their maker and want to be at the center of the universe. Hell is...filled with people who, for all eternity, *still* want to be the center of the universe and who persist in their God-defying rebellion."[20]

In other words, hell is populated with those who want to be there. If the flames and worms are, in fact, literally real, they are likely hardly noticed compared to the suffering of eternal separation from the Creator of good. I can think of no worse fate.

The Means of Reconciliation

Mankind's own choices, at the fall, caused this awful situation in which man was separated from his Maker. In this condition, man lacked connection to the resources of God, so if things had remained the same, he would have had to make his own way. His lack of capacity to understand so many things in his own power would have then, as now, led him to misinterpret a loving God and see Him as cruel and uncaring. But the Creator was

---

[20] D. A. Carson, quoted in E. Gungor, *What Bothers Me Most about Christianity* (New York: Howard Books, 2009), from an interview with Lee Strobel, published in Strobel, *The Case for Christ: A Journalist's Personal Investigation of the Evidence for Jesus* (Grand Rapids: Zondervan, 1998).

not willing to let this state of affairs stand without remedy. Almost immediately after sin first occurred, God introduced death into the world for the first time by killing a small animal to make clothing for the ashamed couple. Physical death became a symbol for spiritual death, or separation from God, and a consequence of the loss of God's sustaining power. After man's heinous crime, no creature would escape physical death ever,[21] because death, by God's decree, is the "wages of sin." Man had sinned, and The *Holy* Judge had decreed that all nature must suffer under the rule of weak and fallible mankind, who had declared himself independent of God. But at the same time, The *Loving* Judge created a remedy for the worst of these consequences: spiritual death (defined as separation from God, the ultimate expression of which is hell). The first animal ever to die was killed by Him, and the wages of sin were symbolically paid. God had immediately instituted a system whereby a lesser creature could substitute for man, and pay his penalty for sin, thereby restoring the relationship between God and man. This was the system of animal sacrifice that remained in place until the advent of Jesus and His work on the cross. God is all powerful and holy, but he is also perfectly just. In the mind of God, actions have consequences (which, again, is why we see it that way as well). We ourselves know that if consequences are not imposed, chaos will result. We do not free those who commit grave crimes from just consequences because such a policy would allow evil to proliferate unabated. This understanding that we possess, like so many others, comes from God. When we rail at God for imposing or allowing just consequences, we are expecting a standard of mercy from God that we do not apply to ourselves.

---

[21] Except for, the Bible records, two Old-Testament characters, and as explained in the New Testament, those who will be alive when Christ returns. (Note: Catholic Christians and some others teach that Mary, the mother of Jesus, was also taken to heaven without dying physically, though this is not recorded in the bible.)

Because of sin, the relationship between God and man is no longer perfect. Through repentance it can be good at times, but because of the current condition of the creation, we will continue to turn away from our Maker. And it will remain this way until, in His perfect timing, He returns to restore the relationship to what it once was. He has promised that at that time he will *"wipe away all tears from [our] eyes; and there shall be no more death, neither sorrow, nor crying, neither shall there be any more pain: for the former things are passed away."* [22]

> *We have by our free choice made our earthly bed. We cannot justly blame God because we lie in it.*

God has allowed us to escape His love if we choose, but neither we nor any part of the universe in which we were placed will escape His justice. We have by our free choice made our earthly bed. We cannot justly blame God because we lie in it.

But because of His mercy, we can be reconciled to him and be considered righteous by the perfect God of the universe, even though we are not. Just as God allowed the first slain animal, a lesser creature, to substitute for Adam and Eve and reconcile them to Him, so our price can be paid through the sacrificial death of a much greater creature, the Son.

---

[22] Revelation 21:4.

Left-Handed Amino Acids: A Small Example of How God Sustains Nature

Thousands of amino acids are known, but only about twenty are used in the proteins that form living organisms. There are two basic structures that amino acids take, and they are mirror images of one another. They are called "left-handed" and "right-handed" based on the direction of their so-called "twist" (Chirality). Anywhere amino acids are found in nature, there is almost always an even mixture of those with a right-handed and those with a left-handed twist. Additionally, all the experiments man has ever done to "build" amino acids in a laboratory have resulted in this even mixture (including the first successful attempt; the famed Miller-Urey experiments of the 1950s). It is nature's strong tendency to form these molecules with evenly mixed Chirality.

The one exception to this rule is that almost all amino acids contained in the proteins of living cells are <u>left-handed only</u>. This is a problem for the naturalist because it is an "unnatural" situation. There is currently no prominent theory as to how this situation could have arisen naturally. The tendency for amino acids to mix evenly in nature is so strong that when an organism dies, part of the decay process is that half of these amino acids return to a right-handed shape. No one has ever postulated a widely accepted reason why the amino acids of living organic tissue should remain left-handed while the creature is alive. Known physical processes should return them to an even mixture in all cells. But if that happened, it would be fatally toxic to life.

Could it be that one reason we are able to exist as living physical beings is that God upholds these structures within our body against their natural tendencies? Science knows of no other reason.

> "…in [God's] hand is the life of every living thing and the breath of all mankind." (Job 12:10)

Chapter Seven

If God Is Real, Why Is Jesus the Only Way to Him?

> *"What then shall I do with Jesus,*
> *who is called the Christ?"*
> —Pontius Pilate

> *"I know men and I tell you that Jesus Christ is no mere man. Between Him and every other person in the world there is no possible term of comparison. Alexander, Caesar, Charlemagne, and I have founded empires. But on what did we rest the creation of our genius? Upon force. Jesus Christ founded His empire upon love; and at this hour millions of men would die for Him."*
> —Napoleon

Accepting Christianity as a correct world view involves more than just answering the question, "Is there really a God?" or working out His attributes. Great multitudes of people across our globe believe fervently that there is a God but do not accept Jesus Christ as any type of manifestation of Him. All widely practiced religions look to a great leader or a group of patriarchs as their source of truth in understanding their world. So why should an objective person in the pursuit of truth prefer one particular historical figure over the others?

The Claims of Christ

The reason, Christians believe, is well stated in this anonymous quote:

> "Buddha never claimed to be God. Moses never claimed to be Jehovah. Mohammed never claimed to be Allah. Yet Jesus Christ claimed to be the true and living God. Buddha simply said, 'I am a teacher in search of the truth.' Jesus said, 'I *am* the Truth.' Confucius said, 'I never claimed to be holy.' Jesus said, 'Who convicts me of sin?' Mohammed said, 'Unless God throws his cloak of mercy over me, I have no hope.' Jesus said, 'Unless you believe in me, you will die in your sins.'"[1]

If I were to have a discussion of the relative merits of the founders of different faiths, it wouldn't have to be a very long one because the issue upon which it turns is unambiguous. Jesus, alone among those who have claimed special spiritual insight over the ages, time and time again, claimed not just to be a repository for the truth about God but to actually *be* God. Indeed, He said that He was the embodiment of truth itself.[2] Unless a person completely rejects the historicity of the gospels—and there is no justification for doing so[3]—there can be no reasonable denial that the man Jesus believed himself to be God. The very nature of that claim requires that everyone who hears it must do something with it. If one is to understand the world outside our senses and the

---

[1] http://onepassiononedevotion.wordpress.com/2009/10/14/jesus-said.
[2] John 14:6.
[3] For a good discussion of the historicity of Jesus, see T. P. Jones, *Conspiracies and the Cross* (Lake Mary, FL: Front Line, 2008).

true nature of things, he must deal with a person who has claimed to be God incarnate.

Leaders of other significant faiths have all been, in most cases by their own admission, one hundred percent human; just people, like you and me, but offering their own unique understanding of fundamental reality for others to either follow or reject. Jesus claimed to be *the founder* of our fundamental reality. The Bible presents him as a fully participating partner in its creation.[4] Furthermore, He claims not just to know the way back to perfect harmony with a holy God, but to *be* that way.[5]

Consider what kind of person would make such a claim. Jesus hasn't been the only one in history to make expansive spiritual claims, but He is the only one who has been taken seriously by billions. As the title of the Dennis Harris novel *Liar, Lunatic or Lord*[6] implies, those who claim to be God must logically fall into one of these three categories. This is because, as logical beings, we know that a thing cannot cause or create itself, so we know that humans cannot be the Creator God. Any human who claims to be must then be insane with self-delusion or have some deceptive or insidious motive for claiming it. So knowing this, we can dismiss out of hand any such claim.

> *Jesus claimed to be the founder of our fundamental reality.*

But wait—if we accept that the physical world is not all that exists in our reality, as I have claimed here, then thorough inquiry requires that we give at least passing consideration to the one remaining possibility. Like it or not, a supernatural explanation could exist. It could be that such a person is more

---

[4] Colossians 1:16.
[5] John 14:6.
[6] This phrase is originally attributed to C. S. Lewis.

than just human. If there is a reality beyond the physical, then such a claimant could actually be who he says he is, even though it does not comport with our experience regarding physical humanness. If one goes as far as to accept the probability that God does exist, then because that admission opens the door to a spiritual reality, he has allowed at least the possibility that Jesus was God incarnate as He said He was. This is the Pandora's Box that, in the mind of the humanist, opens when he allows that there might be a deity or a supernatural designer of some sort. If the universe could in fact have been created and not spontaneously formed, then there could be something outside of nature that an intellectually honest person must explore to the best of his ability. If he does that, the road might lead to an authority that rightfully rules over him, and to the Bible, and to Jesus and to all that he thinks that entails, and he simply doesn't want to go there.

The Atheist Mindset

This is why so many who declare themselves to be humanist or atheist, in my mind, simply mean to say, whether they realize it or not, "I don't want to think this through. I am in charge of my life, and I am not going down a road that may lead me to face the possibility that my life is better handed over to another power, no matter how capable or how loving. I'm not going to end up in some church singing hymns every Sunday. My energies are better spent learning how to deny and ridicule that whole idea and seek the company of those who do the same, so that with luck, I might one day become thoroughly convinced that I am right."

Other skeptics, feeling intellectually forced to admit to a supernatural reality, choose to adopt whatever religious philosophy pleases them. It's fashionable to take elements of various philosophies and create a personal religion that suits.

Take a few spoonfuls of Buddhist enlightenment philosophy, add a cup of New Age spiritualism and mix them in with a few elements of belief in a distant Creator God, and you have a pleasing, non-demanding sort of religious philosophy. Cafeteria religion. It's okay if it's different than the next guy's mixture, because these are "your truths." And the fact that such "truths" are *yours* states the problem clearly; while accepting a spiritual reality, *you* are still in control, and you stand guilty with the rest of us of the original sin.

But contrary to this fashionable thinking, you can't change the truth that way. Truth has nothing to do with what any particular person is convinced of. This book is contra-postmodern. The central theme of it has been that truth exists independently of anything mankind might think or believe. That's why it's so hard to shed oneself of it. Deciding not to face it is often deciding to stop thinking, no matter how much one views oneself as an intellectual or as a spiritually enlightened individual. Sometimes, though, not facing the truth is more the result of limited or misdirected thinking—even over-thinking—imagining anything possible to avoid accepting the truth. But to think openly and to keep searching in an honest way, without bias, is to eventually believe in the God of creation and His word.

Christ's Fulfillment of Prophecy

God's word, the Bible, reports that Jesus was "*the radiance of God's glory and the exact representation of his being.*"[7] Chapter five argued that there are many compelling reasons to believe that the Bible is reliable and authoritative. If one does arrive at the

---

[7] Hebrews 1:3.

conclusion, however tentative, that this amazing record called the Bible must contain the accurate testimony of God's work on earth, then that person must deal with the Bible's claim that Jesus was God. Moreover, the Old Testament portion of this record clearly prophesies the coming of a Christ. This Christ (from the Greek word for "anointed one" and the Greek equivalent of the Hebrew title "Messiah") is the same person referred to as "the seed of the woman" in Genesis 3:15, the "lion of Judah" in Genesis 49:8-10, the "prophet like unto Moses" in Deuteronomy 18:15, "the priest after the order of Melchizedek" in Psalms 110:4, "the branch of Jehovah" in Isaiah 4:2, "Immanuel," the son of a virgin, in Isaiah 7:14, "the rod out of the stem of Jesse" in Isaiah 11:1 and 10 and "the messenger of the covenant" in Malachi 3:1, among many other references. From beginning to end, the record of the history of the world known as the Old Testament forecasts the coming of One sent by the Creator God who would himself be God in the physical form of man.

As with every other subject addressed in scripture, these prophecies have been proved true in later times. One did come, in God's timing, claiming clearly to be the Son of God. A descendent of King David, as prophesied in II Samuel 7:12 and 13, He arrived on the scene of history near the end of the time that the high priesthood was held by the tribe of Judah (which ended with the destruction of the temple in 70 A.D.), as predicted by Jacob, recorded in Genesis 49:10. He was born in Bethlehem, as prophesied in Micah 5:2, and He died sacrificially for us, as foretold in Isaiah 53:5 and Psalms 22:14-18 (the later reference, as I've pointed out, even predicting the casting of lots for His robe). For these and many other reasons, there can be no question that this Jesus was the only one remotely able to claim that He fulfilled these prophecies. No other religious or spiritual leader has ever even claimed to be, nor has anyone else claimed him or her to be, the fulfillment of so much prophecy.

This historical figure, whose existence is recorded by secular writings as well as scriptural ones, did not hesitate to claim deity. His clearest claims to divinity are recorded in the gospel of John. In chapter 14, He says, "*I am the way, the truth, and the life: no man comes to the Father, but by me,*" and in the same chapter, "*he who has seen me, has seen the Father.*" But to me, the most direct claim Jesus ever made that He was God is recorded in chapter 8 and verses 23 and 24 where he says to the Jewish leaders of His time, *"You are from beneath; I am from above. You are of this world; I am not of this world. Therefore I said to you that you will die in your sins; for if you do not believe that I am He, you will die in your sins."* In this statement, Jesus borrows from Jehovah's (a Hebrew name for the Creator God) own words in Isaiah 43, where He says through the prophet over and over again, "I am He!" Clearly, Jesus is using terminology from their own scriptures to make it clear to the Jews who He saw Himself to be. Examples of claims such as these are found throughout the gospels.

So this Messiah, or Christ, whose sacrificial death was clearly predicted by God Himself just moments after original sin[8] and then by several prophets throughout scripture, was perfectly personified in Jesus of Nazareth. Jesus obviously believed He was God, to the point of suffering one of the cruelest capital punishments of all time for His belief.

The Historical Validity of the Resurrection

It is incredibly important to understand that if Christ Jesus is who He said He was and if the Bible accounts are true, then He didn't just suffer our fate on our behalf and let it go at that. He went far beyond that and *conquered* our fate forever by not

---

[8] Genesis 3:15, which speaks prophetically that he (Christ) will bruise your (Satan's) head, and you (Satan) will bruise his (Christ's) heel. This refers to the temporary victory Satan would have at the cross and the permanent victory Christ would have at the resurrection.

staying dead. He showed that death is just one more physical phenomenon under His power and control and that He can choose to allow it or to deny it at His pleasure; this is another attribute possessed only by God, and a symbol of his power over spiritual death as well.

Because this story of resurrection from death implies an ability to control and transcend nature, and because opponents understand the crucial nature of it, atheists and other detractors have, for centuries, seized on it in an attempt to weaken its credibility. And in a human sense, it does indeed seem incredible, so the claims of critics are easily accepted by many. Certainly, though, if Jesus was who He claimed to be, namely the God of creation in human form, then the ability to return from death to life would not be in question, since the Bible ascribes to God all power over nature. But for those who have not yet understood the reliability of God's word and are not yet able to accept it on its face, what is the strictly historical and logical evidence that the account of the most important event in history is true? Did the resurrection really happen?

Like so many things that God has told us, the resurrection account is something that, with an open mind and an accurate world view, we can see the truth of through evidence and reason, independent of faith. Of course, poring over evidence is not necessary since we already know that the resurrection account is true from what we believe to be a reasonable presupposition that God's word can be relied upon whether we can verify it or not. Many Christians would consider a study of the historicity of the resurrection a waste of their valuable time, since they have no personal need to verify it.

> *The only possible explanation for the explosion of Christianity on the pages of human history is the bodily resurrection of Jesus.*

Their faith in God's word is verification enough. And, as we'll discuss in the next chapter, they have the assurance of the Holy Spirit that it is true.

Such faith is surely praiseworthy, but it is clear from the very scripture in which Christians have this faith that it is not the Christian's understanding of the resurrection that is critically at issue. The more important point is that God has told us to be ready to give an answer for what we believe,[9] because it is through us that His Spirit convinces, convicts, and reaches those who do not yet have this faith. If a Christian is to be obedient, he is to seek to master arguments that have the power to convince those who seek truth, but do not yet believe.

The only possible explanation for the explosion of Christianity on the pages of human history is the bodily resurrection of Jesus. Had this not truly happened, there is no way to explain what amounts to the greatest miracle of all—the birth of the church.

The "Swoon Theory"

Over more than two millennia, many philosophers and historians to whom the idea of a bodily resurrection is apparently distasteful have come up with a lot of silly ideas which could be believed only by those who wish them to be true. For instance, the so-called "swoon theory," propagated from the eighteenth century, suggests a conspiracy in which Jesus, supposedly a member of a secret sect, was drugged by Luke (the gospel writer who was a doctor) to protect Him from the brutality of crucifixion. The soldiers who crucified Him were then bribed to accept Jesus' premature feigning of death and bring Him down from the cross. Another conspirator and sect member, Joseph of Arimathea, was enclosed in the cave-tomb

---

[9] I Peter 3:15.

with Jesus, where he revived Him, and at the appointed time, pushed away the stone door while the disciples, dressed in white, frightened away the guards! They then spirited Him away to recover in seclusion while they spread the lie of his resurrection.

My family would tell you that I'm kind of fond of the word "goofy," and if there was ever an application for it, this is it. Acceptance of such an elaborate story, for which there is no evidence at all, requires a staggering suspension of reason. It denies the notorious skill with which the Romans executed people, requires an impossible level of complex conspiracy, and presents a ridiculous picture of a beaten, stabbed and bled-out man, who seemed dead enough to a large crowd of people at the execution site, somehow recovering enough to escape from his burial wrappings (described in detail in scripture), a stone-covered and sealed tomb and an apparently half-witted pair of Roman guards. It is silly enough to be a waste of the paper on which I write it, yet many so-called "liberal Christians" still choose to believe it.

Of course, if this were true, there would still be that sticky problem of what to do with Jesus when He recovered from his "swoon." I assume that most versions of this theory have the conspirators showing Him off a few times in staged presentations of "the risen Lord," and then spiriting Him off someplace never to be seen again, some say to Egypt. It's easy for modern dissimulators to assume the complete ignorance of ancient peoples and get their readers to imagine that this is a reasonable possibility.

This is truly another example in a long list of absurd stories that are presented for us to believe if we are to reject the truth about our reality and declare ourselves the masters of our own lives.

Donald R. Wilson

The Conspiracy Theory

Many simply deny the Bible's account that He rose at all, and instead of trying to explain how all those people might have seen Him, they propose that the whole thing is a fabrication, a conspiratorial story perpetrated by the disciples and the close inner circle of followers. I've read this often from secularists, and it is usually presented as obvious from rigorous historical scholarship. But let's consider the minimum requirements that would have had to be in place for a relatively small group of believers to regale the world with this story of a man returning to life after dying if it didn't really happen.

First, this would have to have started as a conspiracy among at least fifteen to twenty people. All one has to do to realize the implausibility of this is to imagine trying to do it himself. Imagine gathering up fifteen or twenty of your closest friends and trying to get them all to agree on the details of a fabrication that all in the group know will make them complete loons among their peers the minute they tell it. Not an easy thing to do in any time, place or circumstance. But not only would they be thought crazy, these conspirators would also be fully aware that the story would cause them to be accused of body stealing and treated as criminals by two powerful governments. Such a thing would take remarkable planning and rehearsing, and a group discipline unheard of in all the annals of history.

But imagine that you do accomplish this. Besides having to bribe more than a few people outside the group to go along with you, you now have to go out into the world and be so utterly convincing that within decades, tens of thousands will believe. So what was their first step in establishing this level of believability? In a society where women were considered little more than chattel, the word was spread that the first eyewitnesses to this resurrection were a group of women! In that day, women were considered unreliable witnesses and their testimony counted for nothing. Not a great start for such a fantastic story. But despite all this, we find ourselves, twenty centuries later, with billions of people who have no doubt whatsoever that this crazy story was true. Their little ruse somehow became so compelling that it would ultimately change the entire structure of world societies. Because that is what this alleged fabrication did accomplish.

Dinesh D'Souza, in his book *What's So Great About Christianity?*, goes so far as to say this:

> "Christianity is responsible for the way our society is organized and for the way we currently live. So extensive is the Christian contribution to our laws, our economics, our politics, our arts, our calendar, our holidays, and our moral and cultural priorities that historian J.M. Roberts writes, 'We could none of us today be what we are if a handful of Jews nearly two thousand years ago had not believed that they had known a great teacher, seen him crucified, dead, and buried, and then rise again.'"[10]

This appears to have been a little more than just a simple story repeated by a few followers.

There is a record of a staunch Jewish Pharisee who, within a short period after the crucifixion, hated the very idea that this man Jesus might be the promised messiah. He was an avid persecutor of early believers until he had a supernatural encounter with Christ himself. This record is a letter that this

---

[10] Dinesh D'Souza, *What's So Great About Christianity* (Washington, D.C.: Regnery Publishing, 2007), quoting J. M. Roberts, *The Triumph of the West* (London: Little, Brown, 1985).

Pharisee, today known as the apostle Paul to some, Saint Paul to others, wrote to the budding group of believers at Corinth. In the letter, he writes,

> "For I delivered to you as of first importance what I also received, that Christ died for our sins according to the Scriptures, and that He was buried, and that He was raised on the third day according to the Scriptures, and that He appeared to Peter, then to the twelve. After that He appeared to more than five hundred brethren at one time, most of whom remain until now, but some have fallen asleep; then He appeared to James, then to all the apostles. And last of all he was seen of me also, as of one born out of due time." [11]

Now, one may or may not believe that this excerpt from this letter is an accurate narrative of what happened, but it is most certainly a verified historical document that *claims* these things to be true. This writer could not possibly have been a part of the original conspiracy, but that fact is not the strongest evidence here. Paul makes the shocking claim that the risen Christ appeared to more than five hundred people at one time! He further explains that most of them are still around for anyone to find and question; he is saying, *if you don't believe me, ask them for yourself!* Talk about the mother of all conspiracies! It demonstrates the incredible power of wishful thinking that some people could imagine this was a lie.

---

[11] I Corinthians 15:3-8. Note that Paul claims Christ's death and resurrection were "according to the scriptures," thus affirming his belief that Jesus was the fulfillment of Biblical prophecy.

So here we have, only a short period of years after the crucifixion, several hundred people that we know of (the disciples and other close associates of Jesus, the five hundred referenced by Paul and the Corinthian believers to whom Paul writes) who buy into this unbelievable story that a dead man returned to life. Of course, there is much reason to believe that by this time there were actually many more believers than this. This was no trendy belief system made up by a tricky group of charismatic leaders. It was the testimony of fishermen and tax collectors. Thomas Aquinas clearly stated the meaning of this point when he said, "...it would be the most wondrous sign of all if without any wondrous signs the world were persuaded by simple and lowly men to believe things so arduous, to accomplish things so difficult, and to hope for things so sublime."[12] Christianity is a belief system that utterly changed the polytheistic society into which it was born. "...Given how radically at variance Christianity was with the culture it slowly and relentlessly displaced, its eventual victory was an event of such improbability as to strain the very limits of our understanding of historical causality....At [this] particular moment in history...something happened to Western humanity that changed it at the deepest levels of consciousness and at the highest levels of culture."[13]

Moreover, church tradition holds and historical documents partially verify that every original disciple of Jesus would follow in his master's footsteps by being brutally executed for his belief, the only exception being John, who would suffer permanent exile. Paul himself would be beheaded. If this is true, what possible motivation could have incited these men to maintain a bizarre fraud until they were executed for it? Many

---

[12] T. Aquinas, *Summa Contra Gentiles*, as quoted in W. L. Craig, *Reasonable Faith: Christian Truth and Apologetics* (Wheaton, IL: Crossway Books, 2008).

[13] David Hart, *Atheist Delusions, The Christian Revolution and its Fashionable Enemies* (New Haven, CT: Yale University Press, 2009).

have died for causes or beliefs in which they were sincerely deluded. But men don't willingly die to maintain what they *know* to be a lie. How contagious the disease of madness must have been in first century Palestine. The only reason for these things, to my mind, is that the man Jesus really did return from the dead.

> *Men don't willingly die to maintain what they know to be a lie.*

Other Weak and Wishful Explanations

Beginning very early after His resurrection, some claimed that Jesus' body was stolen by his followers or that the religious or Roman leaders had moved it to prevent just such an occurrence. The idea that His followers took His body is ludicrous in view of the Roman guards who were placed there to guard it. His followers had no power to overcome such an obstacle, and had they found some way to succeed, they would have been hunted down by the Roman authorities. Matthew 28 does record an effort by the Jewish authorities to make this claim, and it was apparently widely believed among the Jews, but it's clear from the passage that the whole reason for making the claim is that the Jewish leaders *believed* that this powerful miracle-worker did, in fact, rise from the dead.

There is no evidence anywhere in secular or Biblical history that the local or Roman leaders had any motivation to move Jesus' body. Though the Jewish leaders had asked Pontius Pilate to post guards, no one in Palestine was afraid of Jesus' followers. As far as anyone could see, His movement had been thoroughly defeated and His followers scattered. If they had moved the body, the authorities would certainly have presented it early on as a means of putting an end to this upstart movement.

With all of the above efforts failing, determined secularists have turned to attacking the records of the whole affair, saying that the

New Testament texts were written decades or even generations after the death of the supposed eyewitnesses and that the idea of a bodily resurrection was never imagined until then. But honest scholarship does not support this idea. Any reasonable review of the manuscript evidence supports a completion of the four Gospels well before the end of the first century (John's gospel being the last), when many of the eyewitnesses were still alive.

These and other "theories" have been massaged and modified over time to try to make them more believable. But they are no different than any other of the elaborate ideas man has invented to avoid facing the truth of scripture (Darwinian evolution and other naturalist theories included). Many of these fantasies are laughable to an honest, thoughtful person, but the sad truth is that people of this description are hard to come by in our more-and-more secularized society.

Finally, perhaps the most compelling reason that the story of the resurrection could not have been fabricated is the presence, right there in the local area where the story began, of the tomb. It is recorded in secular histories as well as the Bible that Jesus was crucified by the Romans publicly and buried in the tomb of a man named Joseph of Arimathea. Jesus was widely known among the local people because of His very public ministry and it was known to almost everyone where He was buried. If someone wanted to know if the story was true, all they had to do was go have a look at the empty tomb! Although the Bible doesn't record it, I believe that this may have been exactly what many did do and that the rolled-away stone was for some time one of the most powerful igniters of the flame of Christianity in Palestine.

> *Without the resurrection, the Christian faith is unremarkable.*

Jesus was one of a number of messiah-candidates, you might say, that came along during this period in Jewish history.

All of the others had disciples, and all of them died. When they were gone, no one imagined that they had been raised from the dead. Their disciples scattered and flocked to other teachers, and their movements died with them. Were it not for the resurrection, and the ability of the populace to believe it really happened, Christianity would have suffered the same fate. Without the resurrection, the Christian faith is unremarkable. Something made the resurrection not only believable but compelling to the people in whose time it occurred. The tenacity of this belief system, the importance of crushing it to its detractors, its historical longevity and its popularity among world cultures is explainable only by the credibility of the resurrection account as the detonator of the greatest movement in world history.

The Critical Importance of the Resurrection

It is said that the late New York Senator James Donovan was once involved in a debate over the merits of capital punishment. Caught up in the fervor of the discussion, he made his point by asking, "Where would Christianity be if Jesus got eight to fifteen years, with time off for good behavior?"[14]

Where indeed would it be? It is this resurrection story, this conquering and defeating of death, that is the linchpin of the Christian faith. It is what gave history's most successful movement its impetus and its meaning. We are promised that because this Jesus overcame the just penalty for our rebellion and returned to life, we can overcome it also by simply accepting His death as a

As a fully human person, Jesus provided a link between the spiritual world and the physical one.

---

[14] www.anecdotage.com.

substitute for the penalty we should rightly face. Because He lives, we will live also. If we decide, by our free choice, to accept this gift, the true *us*, our soul, will not have to suffer permanent separation from God. Death no longer has power over us. Christ's sacrificial death satisfies God's perfect justice and the resurrection demonstrates that our life is eternal—that physical death is merely a portal through which we must pass. Without the reality of the resurrection, there is no Christianity.

As a fully human person, Jesus provided a link between the spiritual world and the physical one. He was God experiencing humanness. And as a human, He was responsible in Adam for the rift in the relationship between a Holy God and us. He existed on both sides of the chasm. Once Jesus had miraculously entered the womb of a human female, the guilt of humanity was as much His as it is ours. But He lived the human life as it was intended to be lived; sinlessly. His life, death and resurrection closed the gap forever and gave us contact again with our Father. The just penalty has been paid. In Adam, we are separated from God. In Christ, sometimes called the "last Adam," a conduit is opened for us to be joined again with Him.

If only we, as creatures in God's image, could fully understand that this is a perfect example of what love does. When a relationship is broken, it cannot be mended by one person. There is a cost to be paid when two people have been separated by any act which has damaged the rapport that existed between them. There is a level of suffering that must be experienced, and this is the natural price of repairing the relationship. If one loves another person as God loves us, he is willing to pay this price by opening the door to reconciliation. This is never done painlessly. And of course, it is only half the solution. The other person must choose to walk through the door.

Because the structure of the relationships that we experience is a reflection of the structure of God's perfect love, we should not be surprised to find that being reconciled to Him requires an active choice on our part to pass through this conduit that He has opened in the sacrificial death of the God-man, Jesus. Because of what He has done, we *can be* reconciled to Him. But as I've pointed out, authentic love requires each party to choose it. In Jesus' words:

> *"Behold, I stand at the door and knock; if anyone hears My voice and opens the door, I will come in to him and will dine with him, and he with Me."* [15]

Clearly, He wants us back. He suffered the pain caused by our rebellion and paid the price of our sin. We suffer that pain as well. All that's left is one small act; a choice to open the door and restore things to the way they were meant to be. Believe, accept, internalize, and act on all that is laid out in this awesome saga of history and live as full, rich and truly successful a life as is possible on this fallen earth, followed by an eternal close fellowship with God as it was always intended to be. Or choose *yourself*, and enjoy the best life you can, followed by eternal separation from Him, as it was never intended. It will always be a free choice of every person, because in His perfect wisdom, God knew it could not work any other way.

This is the logic of the Christian faith. God exists, because there is no escaping the powerful evidence, both internal and external, that He must exist. With mercy, patience, wisdom and justice that often rises to a level we can't understand, He controls everything, because He owns everything. He wishes to love and commune with His highest creation, mankind. He has given us sufficient information and reasoning ability to understand our world, and He delights in our discovery of it. But He will always be greater than His creation, so we will never

---

[15] Revelation 3:20.

approach a full understanding of everything. Faith in Him will always remain necessary.

The Bible, whose reliability is supported by evidence far more complete and compelling than that of any other ancient history, records that God set up creation to facilitate a relationship between Himself and man. But man thought better of it and rebelled, ruining the plan. Knowing about this rebellion from outside of time, God made a plan to restore man to Himself by taking the form of His creation and suffering once and for all the just penalty for that rebellion. Beyond just suffering this penalty, He went on to conquer it and remove its sting forever. Still wanting the best for man, He offers restoration of the relationship and the wonderful benefits that spring from it as a free choice available to every man. It's clear from His word that He waits, and hopes that none will "perish, but that all will come to repentance."[16]

N. T. Wright, Anglican Bishop and powerful defender of Christianity, has put it this way:

> "The need which the Christian faith answers is not so much that we are ignorant and need better information, but that we are lost and need someone to come and find us, stuck in the quicksand waiting to be rescued, dying and in need of new life.
>
> "...With Jesus, God's rescue operation has been put into effect once and for all. A great door has swung open in the cosmos which can never again be shut. It's the door to the prison where we've been kept chained up. We are

---

[16] 2 Peter 3:9.

offered freedom: freedom to experience God's rescue for ourselves…We are all invited—summoned actually—to discover, through following Jesus, that this new world is indeed a place of justice, spirituality, relationship, and beauty, and that we are not only to enjoy it as such but to work at bringing it to birth on earth as in heaven. *In listening to Jesus, we discover whose voice it is that has echoed around in the hearts and minds of the human race all along.*"[17]

It can't be said much better than that.

---

[17] N.T. Wright, *Simply Christian* (New York: Harper-Collins, 2000).

Chapter Eight

What Makes Christians So Sure They Have It Right?

I admire the serene assurance of those who have religious faith. It is wonderful to observe the calm confidence of a Christian with four aces.
—Mark Twain

The previous chapter closed with a quote from N. T. Wright that began with the observation that Christianity's power is *not* in providing superior information so that we can understand our world well enough to judge the belief system reasonable. To think that it is the duty of a Christian to overpower the objections of unbelievers with the power of evidence for the faith would be a misunderstanding of the role of apologetics and a distortion of the relationship between man and God. What has been said thus far has not been an effort to invite the reader to *decide* whether or not the Christian faith is a valid understanding of reality. Such an approach implies, as has been pointed out in earlier chapters, that it is the proper place of a created being to judge his Creator. Instead, the foregoing chapters have been intended to lay out the *rational foundation* for faith in Christ.

There is a difference. The former offers up Christianity for mankind's verdict. The latter is explanatory of the rational basis for trusting the inherent truth of Christianity that much of fallible mankind has missed.

The Power, and the Impotence, of Apologetics

Any reader who tends toward atheism or agnosticism and who has read this far is not convinced by any power of the arguments that have been presented here. That's simply because these arguments have no power to overcome the reluctance of one who is not truly seeking the truth. Let's face it. Most of these arguments are inductive—that is, they only render a conclusion that is *likely* true, not proven true in the deductive sense.[1] The best result a philosophical argument can achieve is to make it *more likely* that a reader would accept it as true than it would have been before he considered it. The Bible is clear throughout that *"men love darkness rather than light,"*[2] and because of that, no person has the capacity within himself to reach an adequate understanding of the full and complete nature of his reality anyway (I Corinthians 2:14[3]). So arguing logically for the faith will not, in its own power, bring a confirmed doubter to an understanding of the folly of his world view.

> *No person has the capacity within himself to reach an adequate understanding of the full and complete nature of his reality.*

A well-known U.S. television pundit of our time has coined

---

[1] Let it not be forgotten that this is also true of opposing arguments.
[2] John 3:19.
[3] *"The man without the Spirit does not accept the things that come from the Spirit of God, for they are foolishness to him, and he cannot understand them, because they are spiritually discerned."*

the slogan, "The spin stops here!"[4] Well, the truth is that among human opinions, the spin never stops, and it will always be possible, even easy, for humankind to avoid facing these truths. This ability to "spin" reality is part of the freedom God has granted his highest creation. If we apply the same approach to "deciding" whether or not Christianity is true that we apply to deciding our political party affiliation, we quickly get lost in the "spin" of strong opinion about the issue. The only way to stop the spin, whether in politics or faith, is to learn every single fact, nuance, piece of background information, piece of evidence and the ideas and motivations of every person concerned, both present and past, in order to unravel for ourselves the truth of the many issues involved. This is, of course, a completely unreasonable goal and even if we were to achieve it, we would still face the obstacle of our own personal limitations, presuppositions and agendas. So, in politics, we do our best to align ourselves with those that seem most in line with our philosophy and version of common sense and hope it works out. With regard to the supremely important matters of faith, though, hoping for the best won't do. We need something more than reason.

In my introduction, I mentioned that few people even try to unravel the complicated truths about life. They either adopt someone else's truth or make one up for themselves and press on. The difficulty of un-spinning the opinions of men is certainly one of the reasons for that phenomenon. But it is a profoundly unsatisfying solution. As I've spent so much time pointing out, we already know enough, just by the force of our natural instincts and what we see around us, to know that we are "lost and need someone to come and find us."[5] We know that

---

[4] Bill O'Reilly, Fox News.
[5] Wright, *Simply Christian*.

we are fallible, weak, unreasonable, selfish and unwise creatures, though some battle daily to convince themselves otherwise. Most unsettlingly, the secularist believes that the menacing cloud of permanent obliteration hangs over him every day of his life, and he is not ignorant of the implications of his belief. So, people try to lose themselves in diversion from this reality instead of seeking to master an understanding of it. This is the driving force behind the huge success of the entertainment and leisure industries of our world and why they remain growth industries. The fear of facing this truth is the main reason for the reluctance to discuss these issues that most highly-secularized people display, and it is often the real motivation for the malevolent attitudes they brandish when these matters are raised. They simply don't want to think about it. We need rescue from the despair that naturally arises from the cynical view of reality that we are taught at every turn.

As Wright pointed out, this is the need that Christianity answers. Apologetics, or reason, is capable of laying a foundation for that rescue, of creating an intellectual environment suitable for it to take place. But because in the end it is just probabilities and opinions based on propositions of arguable veracity, it has limited power to "stop the spin" and get us to a full understanding of what is real. The incredible "truth book," the Word of God, is right again when it says, *"The mind set on the flesh is hostile to God, it does not submit to God's law, <u>nor can it do so</u>."* [6] Mankind needs more.

The Final Piece of the Truth Puzzle

The previous pages have hopefully laid out the way in which truth is properly understood in a human sense. We have only two places in our limited sphere to find it: the revealed truth of

---

[6] Romans 8:7. Underlining added.

God himself, and what we are able to reason out from that revealed truth. We have seen that revelation and reason are incomplete, but that they are complete enough to lead us to faith that God is powerful enough to be in control of what we don't know. But even if these things are accepted intellectually, we are still short something. That something is *assurance*. How do we *know* that we are not accepting viewpoints that are simply spun in a convincing way? How do we know that our emotions are not overpowering our minds when we are inclined to believe these precepts? As I've asked before in these pages, how can we know we've finally gotten to the truth? And how can we reach the point of confident faith in it?

> *...even if these things are accepted intellectually, we are still short something. That something is assurance.*

As the earthly work of the God-man Jesus was coming to a conclusion and He prepared to exit physical life on His own terms, He reassured His followers that they would not be left alone:

> *"And I will pray the Father, and he shall give you another Comforter, that he may abide with you forever; even <u>the Spirit of truth</u>; whom the world cannot receive, because it seeth him not, neither knoweth him: but ye know him; for he dwelleth with you, and shall be in you."*[7]

Jesus said that His physical presence on this earth would be replaced by the spiritual presence of a "Comforter" that would have the power to convict, convince and assure men of the

---

[7] John 14:16-17. Underlining added.

truth. But quite shockingly, our Lord said plainly that "the world"[8] would not only reject this Comforter, but that it would not even be *capable* of accepting Him! The logical question that arises from this statement then, is, "How is it that Christians are able to accept this Comforter?"

The answer is that Christians have been through a process of change that unbelievers have not. Notice that Jesus said that the world will reject this Comforter, "but ye know him," referring to His disciples and other followers. Those men and women, like today's Christians, were no different than any other person who has lived throughout history, or will live in the future. Like us, they lived and died under the curse of sin, in their own power confused, unsure and generally imperfect (as many atheists so enjoy pointing out). But in one way those followers were different. *Because they sincerely wanted to know the truth about reality, whatever it was, they were fundamentally changed when confronted with it.* And it is because of this change that occurs in the minds and souls of people who are truly open to truth that these men were able to receive the assurance of the Comforter in their lives.

This is still the way conversion works today. One doesn't *decide* intellectually that the preponderance of evidence makes Christianity plausible and give up her objections because she has *judged* the belief system worthy. She may do that, but it is not assured faith in Christ. The human mind is weak and wavering and making a judgment about Christianity in an academic bubble, so to speak, only sets up the opportunity for secular reasoning to burst the bubble. Because such a decision is based on human reason only, it is vulnerable to being caught up in the spin of other human thought.

But this Comforter Jesus promised—the Holy Spirit of God—knows the true motives and desires of every person. Part

---

[8] Bible writers often refer to unbelievers as "the world."

of His mission is to convict and convince men that it is not their intellect that will save them but their recognition of their true state of affairs as fallen creatures and their honest desire to be back where they were always intended to be: in a close and loving relationship with their Creator. In the person of the Holy Spirit, God reminds, prompts, prods and assures His sons and daughters of their deep need for this re-connection with their Creator.

Many are not listening to this voice. Some have shut it out permanently and will never again hear it. These are the ones who cannot receive, cannot see and cannot know the Comforter. Those of them that began reading this book have stopped reading long before they reached this chapter.

What has been laid out in this book shows that faith in God and Christ is reasonable, but this reasonableness only makes it possible for us to listen with confidence to the prompting of the Holy Spirit. We all know we must choose. No one escapes it. A free choice must be made by every person who is gifted with enough of life to reach an age and mental capacity where they are able to understand the voice that they continually hear. This is what Wright meant in saying that "in listening to Jesus, we discover whose voice it is that has echoed around in the hearts and minds of the human race all along."[9]

Ultimately, faith stands on the assurance of the Comforter—the Holy Spirit—in our lives. This is why Christians are able to be fully confident in their faith even when they don't understand a single point made in this book. If a person has truly experienced salvation, he or she knows the truth because

> *Ultimately, faith stands on the assurance of...the Holy Spirit in our lives.*

---

[9] Wright, *Simply Christian*.

the Comforter continually reinforces the truth with gentle reminders and urgings. If you think about it, it makes sense that God designed things this way. Think of the massive amount of research, reasoning and long consideration that is required to build a case for Christianity intellectually. Besides the fact that if the way to Christ was through reason, we could never have full assurance, it would also be a very long journey. We would have no young believers at all, and many would die unsaved along the road to full academic understanding. A huge number over the ages, because of disabilities, could never understand and would have no hope. Even when such an understanding was reached, it would always be vulnerable to the spin of human interpretation. And most offensive of all, the higher a person's intelligence the better chance he would have of salvation. But God, in His typical, clever-beyond-description way, created in us a certain innate understanding about Himself and reinforced that understanding with the testimony of His amazing physical universe. This is enough, He tells us, to eliminate any excuse we think we might have for not knowing Him. But not stopping with "enough," the Creator stepped into His handiwork and demonstrated personally how a successful life is lived, then followed with the affirming comfort of His Holy Spirit. Rather than allowing us to benefit from pride in our pittance (by comparison) of intellect, He made it of no importance at all! In fact, He has strongly warned that it can easily get in the way. If we are truly interested in knowing the transcendent truth about our reality, we have, regardless of our intellectual ability, everything we need and more.

Though Mark Twain meant it sarcastically in the opening quote of this chapter, mature, informed Christians really are playing the game of life with four aces. They have the "calm confidence" that Twain referred to because they have the assurance of the Holy Spirit that what they know of reality through revelation, reason, and faith is the clearest, sharpest view possible of the fallen world that surrounds them. It is predictable that to the skeptic this would look like escapism, because at its heart, Christianity is experiential and the skeptic has not experienced it. But the skeptic is no different than any other person. He hears—or at least has heard—the still, small voice like the rest of us, and if he sincerely begins to look for its source, he will find it in Christ Jesus.

Chapter Nine

What about This, and What about That?

"Sometimes I lie awake at night, and ask, 'Where have I gone wrong?' Then a voice says to me, 'This is going to take more than one night.'"
—Charlie Brown

Anyone who has read this far, truly seeking to understand Christianity as a belief system, likely has many questions and comments. Most of those who are distrustful of Christianity come to this point with a lifetime of objections, talking points and issues spilling over in their minds regarding what's been said in this book and many other places. Thoughtful Christians also want to know more. So, in closing, I am going to exercise my author's prerogative to digress a little and touch on a number of points. In the body of this work, I have covered what I think are the essential issues related to faith in a Creator God and the reasonableness of Christianity as a belief system. In the process, I've touched on a number of common objections that cause people to be cautious in drawing closer to this world view. But there is much out there that is misunderstood and incorrect regarding the essence of Christianity, its history and so forth, and some of this has resulted in some well-worn canards and shallow or fallacious arguments employed in books, articles, religion or atheism forums and on the streets everywhere. But on the other hand, there are also many fair, legitimate questions that arise in the minds of those who have a real desire to know. This chapter is intended to be a small step toward answering just a few of those questions.

But there are so many! What about the idea of the Trinity?[1] What about miracles? What about saints, dependence on church tradition and denominational differences? What about other forms of spirituality? What about all those seemingly meaningless liturgies and weird worship practices? What about those overdressed and overdone evangelists, healers and singers on television? What about all the constraints Christianity puts on one's lifestyle? What about all these "conflicts" with scientific discoveries? What about so-and-so, who says such-and-such about Christianity? What about this, and what about that?

Obviously, each and every question that arises from this discussion cannot be answered in one relatively short book. If they could, we authors could all put up our pens and do something else. The questions in the paragraph above suggest dozens of book ideas, and they have in fact inspired hundreds, I'm sure. This particular book, however, is an effort to distill one Christian's understanding of the Christian world view into an outline of its *essential* teachings about reality and not to exhaustively defend every possible ramification of it. There are good answers to the questions above, and it would certainly be a worthy pursuit to find them, but in doing that, it's easy to get off track. Although these issues may bother you, irritate you, fascinate you or frustrate you, none of them are essential to the

---

[1] See appendix A for a short discussion of the Trinity.

core question of whether or not Christianity is a reasonable, rational world view. This one question is the vital issue that must be resolved first, before one deals with the rest of the questions and perceived problems that arise from it. See the recommended further reading at the end of this book if you wish to pursue more answers.

A Few Sticking Points

Nonetheless, I do want to commit just a few pages to expanding upon some of the main sticking points that I hear quite often from those who cannot bring themselves to accept Christianity as a belief system. Many of these issues tend to trip up believers as well, and this chapter is for you, too. My intent is not to present a one-sided argument in a forum where no one can argue with me. It is rather to acknowledge my respect for the difficulty of getting good answers to some of the most important questions we human beings could ever ask. So, I'll revisit briefly some issues we kind of breezed over in the previous chapters, and touch on a couple of new ones.

I respect and appreciate those among us who at least see the importance of finding rational answers to these crucial questions and actively seek to do so, whether they agree with me or not. Some of the most stimulating conversations I've ever had have been with self-described atheists, doubters, and those who follow other belief systems who probe my faith with reasonable, insightful questions. I am grateful for these people in my life. No one should equate forcefully presenting arguments for one's belief system with considering people of different beliefs to be fools. As I'll discuss in a few paragraphs, to be truly tolerant is to respect the God-given right

If the Bible is false in any degree, then we have no idea to what degree it may be true.

of others to believe what they wish, while not retreating from the truth ourselves.

The Authority of Scripture

The most important attacks that are made against Christianity are attacks against the accuracy and authority of scripture. In chapter five, I discussed pretty thoroughly the reasons why I believe the Christian Bible can be trusted as true. I did this, and I mention it again here, because it is the absolutely critical foundation of the Christian faith. The writings accepted by the Christian faith as inspired by the Creator God must be not only rationally defensible but thoroughly compelling to an unbiased, judicial mind if Christianity is to be accepted as a true belief system. If the Bible is false in any degree, then we have no idea to what degree it may be true, and the Christian belief system stands only on the ifs, ands and buts of human reason. Scholars are then free to pick and choose what is true and what is not, and the roles of God and man are effectively reversed, feeding nicely into the hands of atheist philosophy. Atheists seem to know instinctively that if you crack this foundation on which Christianity is built, the beliefs, tenets and doctrines of the entire world view will tumble in on themselves like a skyscraper being razed for new construction. Many of the Christians in the world, though, don't seem to get this. *There can be no mistake; the Bible must be accurate from the first verse to the last in order for the belief system of Christianity to make sense as a valid statement of human reality.* The whole of Christianity is based upon the Bible being correct, and if it is wrong in its description of reality in any way, from creation to genealogy to the role of Christ to the resurrection, then the tenets on which I base my life are, as John MacArthur put it, merely "fluctuating religious sentiment."[2] It is crucial to

---

[2] MacArthur, *The Truth War*.

realize that, for the reasons I discussed in chapter five and for countless other reasons, the Bible can be relied upon to present absolute, transcendent truth about our world. We have only to look at it in context and with a mind set on finding truth to develop an accurate view of the world.

The Exclusivity of the Christian Claim to Truth

Another common complaint about Christianity is its claim of exclusivity. In the current Western culture of inclusiveness and tolerance, we tend to commit the very human error of taking a good thing to extremes. Inclusiveness and tolerance are wonderful virtues (taken from and based on Biblical teaching, by the way), but our culture has gone far beyond tolerance and inclusiveness. There is a difference between tolerance of something and accepting it as true. As a matter of fact, the word *tolerance* implies a difference of opinion between those tolerating each other. Living in harmony with and giving respect to those with whom we disagree is tolerance. Including them in our circle of friendship and our civic processes is inclusiveness.

> *If a person makes a claim that Christianity is wrongheaded because it excludes other faiths, that person is himself making an exclusive claim.*

Neither of these remotely implies accepting their beliefs as true. In fact, the Bible requires Christians to go further and not only to tolerate and include all people they encounter but to deal with them in Christian love as well. Modern culture would have us believe that in order to be tolerant, we have to view positions contrary to our own as of equal value with ours. We even hear that these are "other people's truths," and that it is arrogant to view ours as more true than theirs. This claim is plainly self-defeating, as I have pointed out earlier, because claiming that truth is relative is an absolute truth-claim itself. Since that violates the logical principal of non-contradiction, it is nonsense.

Different faiths make opposing claims. In chapter seven, I discussed the fact that Jesus claimed to be the only way to God. Every major religion besides Christianity would deny that claim. Christians are required by the truth of God's word to gently and respectfully point out, resist and correct error wherever they find it (including, and most importantly, when they find it among their own). All major religions make mutually exclusive claims and all religions make claims contrary to atheism and agnosticism in their various forms. The truth is that *all world views claim exclusivity, including atheism.* As I said previously, if a person makes a claim that Christianity is wrongheaded because it excludes other faiths, that person is himself making an exclusive claim. It is more of the type of self-defeating argument that humanists must make in order to defend their positions. The point has been made more than once in this book that truth is not something that is personal. There is no point complaining that Christianity disrespects other "truths." There is not a menu of truths to choose between. Since truth is truth, and Christianity claims to be God's illumination of it, there is no reason to be surprised that it is an exclusive claim.

Historical Science and the Bible

Probably the most formidable barrier honest people encounter to accepting Biblical history in our time is the relentless insistence of the secular culture that the Bible's history does not jibe with modern science. I have a number of Christian friends whose reasoning I respect a great deal who are unable to stand against the idea that the earth is billions of years old, for instance, because of the persistent assertion of secular science that this is essentially proved. "Religion" sections of bookstores are rife with volumes written by bright and powerful Christian authors attempting to explain how, in describing creation, God really meant to say that He did it in exactly the same way that twenty-first century scientists would one day say He did.

I made it clear in my introduction that I have no intention of digressing into a discussion of evolution and the age of the earth in detail, because these questions open up issues of just about every scientific and historical discipline imaginable, and the specifics simply cannot be covered in what is intended to be a concise statement of beliefs. I leave that to others. But of course, it is on the minds of virtually every person today, whether they agree or not, that science now unabashedly claims to have "discovered" that the Genesis account of creation cannot be true because the earth and universe are without doubt billions of years old and biological evolution is a proven fact.

My answer to this criticism is a simple one: science has "discovered" no such thing. As I have indicated previously in this work, biological evolution and a billions-of-years-old universe are the wishful thinking of a vocal (to say the least) segment of mankind that wishes to establish a basis for eliminating God. These theories are based on a modicum of science blended with expansive imaginations and employing scores of rescue theories[3] and special pleadings.[4]

I can hear the secularist replying in the usual condescending way that this is another example of an uneducated Christian stubbornly closing his eyes and ears to the truth. I want to

---

[3] A *rescue theory* is a theory devised to "rescue" another theory that has been shown to have problems. All (and I do mean all) of the major secular theories addressing the origin of the universe and of life employ many layers of rescue theories in an attempt to "patch up" problems with the main theory or to adjust another rescue theory.

[4] A *special pleading* arbitrarily exempts the person arguing a point from standards or rules the arguer applies to others.

briefly address this theme that we hear so often from today's elitists. Critics often feel justified in using words like *uneducated*, even when they have no knowledge of the educational qualifications of the person in question because they, whether highly educated themselves or not, believe so wholeheartedly in what they have been taught about these subjects that they believe their education must surely trump that of anyone who disagrees with it. What I think comforts them most is the fact that most of their friends believe the same things, so they feel justified in this unsubstantiated, arbitrary claim. How often have we heard that no educated person denies evolution anymore? But the problem with education is that it is permeated with this lie. It may be true that no educated person, *who has accepted the poorly-substantiated claims of some of his courses,* denies evolution anymore. But the first role of education in our society should be to teach students to think for themselves and hold up everything they are taught against the backdrop of logic, common sense and full disclosure. Instead, in this area of inquiry especially, our education system is set up to support a bizarre version of historical possibilities, while obscuring many contrary facts and suppressing free thinking.

This particular kind of attack really arises from more than just a desire to denigrate an opposing viewpoint by attacking its proponent's qualifications (known in logic as an *ad hominem* argument.) It arises from the hubris of believing oneself either in the majority or among the elite. I have pointed out repeatedly that the fundamental barrier between God and man is man's arrogance. My experience has been that many of those who have rejected God completely consider themselves uniquely intelligent, placing human reason (specifically theirs) above God's revelation.

> *Reason is properly used to understand revelation, not to modify or correct it.*

Again, I have spent much time here supporting the idea that transcendent truth does exist in our world. I can't overemphasize the importance of this to the Christian faith. If something is true by the dictionary definition,[5] then it is in no way affected by any opinion of one man, of all of mankind or of any size majority in between. Truth is not modified, even slightly, by the opinions of the self-appointed elite among men, no matter their education or qualifications. It is so important that Christians understand and internalize this idea. Our faith cannot be sustained if we deify human reason. I said in chapter three that revelation must outrank reason because reason is a gift possessed by fallible, created creatures, while revelation is the declaration of an infallible, omniscient Creator. Reason is properly used to understand revelation, not to modify or correct it.

However, many of us have allowed human reason to be placed above God's revelation to us. We do this because of the very kind of attacks mentioned above. If we hear often enough that highly-educated scientists and professors believe that Christianity is an intellectual absurdity, and if news anchors, authors and huge numbers of ordinary citizens chime in their agreement for long enough, many of us are eventually seduced into believing that what The Creator has clearly said must be modified to bring it in line with the beliefs of the majority of those whom He created. It is a silly idea, but such is the power of mob mentality. Confronting it and standing up to it is a burden many Christians, often including those who would be seen as important theologians, are unwilling to bear.

The argument, while we're on the subject, is not between faith and science, as is so often claimed. Secular viewpoints usually try to characterize it this way, and I see many Christian writings that

---

[5] Webster's Dictionary and Thesaurus (Nichols Publishing Group, 1999): "in accordance with reality or fact."

What about This, and What about That?

buy into this by trying to defend faith as existing in a separate domain from that of science. Science explains how, faith explains why—no need for argument. This sounds like a reasonable approach: an explanation that keeps science in its box, and faith in its place. If we could all just look at it this way, we'd all get along, right? Unfortunately, there are many subjects in which faith *does* explain how. The essential error here is that this statement is an invalid comparison of two dissimilar things. *How can faith explain why if it's utterly wrong about how?* Jesus himself asked us this question when he said, *"If I told you earthly things and you do not believe, how will you believe if I tell you heavenly things?"*[6] It is true that faith is not specifically in the business of science and that science has little to do with faith. But the argument about our pre-history was never between faith and science. *The argument is between one approach to science and another.* It is between science based on an intelligible world view versus science based on an unintelligible one. It is between science conducted with a mind open to all reasonable possibilities versus science that has limited itself to strictly natural explanations, science that openly examines and presents all evidence versus science that shuts down discussion and suppresses evidence. And as I've worked so hard to explain, the argument is between science that honors God's Word and science that presupposes the absence of God.

The Bible represents the truth about our reality. True scientists begin with that understanding. There are parts of the Bible that are difficult to understand fully and correctly without diligent study and knowledge of the historical setting and the original languages used. This is what keeps preachers and theologians in business. But most parts, including those parts related to the crucial issues of our faith, are written plainly and clearly, using ordinary rules of communication by the written

---

[6] John 3:12.

word. This manifesto, for instance, does not require years of study by Ph.D. scholars to understand what is written in it and intended by it, whether or not one agrees with it. It employs ordinary language understood all over the English-speaking world. The Bible is no different in its essential character. It should be read in the same way one would read a modern book of any kind, and its plain meaning, in context, should be accepted as such. With this in mind, it should be the basis for all our thinking, including scientific inquiry.

The "D" Word

As an example of this, it is unwise for Christians who are uneasy about having no place on the bandwagon of popular scientific opinion to appeal to escape devices like the all-too-common practice of reinterpreting the word *day* in Genesis 1. There are a number of problems with this kind of attempt at reconciling man's opinion with God's declaration of truth, not the least of which is the order of creation given in the scripture versus the one given by evolutionism.

The first thing to understand on this issue is that the very idea that *day* does not mean an ordinary twenty-four hour day in Genesis 1 has no support whatsoever in any commonly used method of understanding language. The only reason anyone would try to read more into the word than its plain meaning would be to try to force it to comply with some philosophical mindset about the past. We have no trouble interpreting the word *day*, even though it can mean several different types of time periods or points in time, in any other part of scripture. When the word occurs, we automatically know what it means because we don't apply any preconception to it. The early chapters of Genesis are clearly a narrative historical record, explaining what happened at creation in sequential terms. It is not at all poetic in form or structure. Were it not for the crushing pressure on our minds of the old-earth paradigm, we would not spend a moment asking ourselves what *day* really meant. In reality, all these attempts at forcing the Bible's narrative to comply with man's ideas make Christians look foolish, since it is obvious to those same secularists whose favor they crave that *day*, in the context of the passage, obviously means an ordinary day.

The Absolute Criticality of Accepting the Plain Meaning of Genesis

The more important problem, though, is that if, in fact, the time line described by the Creator does align with the one discovered (supposedly) by His upstart created ones, then the entire basis of Christianity falls to ruin. Again, leading atheists seem to understand this, while it is lost on many leading theologians. G. Richard Bozarth, an atheist, shows his clear understanding of what's at stake here when he writes:

> "Christianity is, must be, totally committed to the special creation as described in Genesis and Christianity must fight with its full might, fair or foul, against the theory of evolution. It becomes clear now that the whole justification of Jesus' life and death is predicated on the existence of Adam and the forbidden fruit he and Eve ate. Without the original sin, who needs to be redeemed? Without Adam's fall into a life of constant sin terminated by death, what purpose is there to Christianity? None.
>
> "Christianity has fought, still fights, and will fight science to the desperate end over

> evolution, because evolution destroys utterly and finally the very reason Jesus' earthly life was supposedly made necessary. Destroy Adam and Eve and the original sin, and in the rubble you will find the sorry remains of the son of god. Take away the meaning of his death [sic]. If Jesus was not the redeemer who died for our sins, and this is what evolution means, then Christianity is nothing!"[7]

When my children were teenagers, they might have responded to the reading of this passage with the exclamation, "Duh!" This passage is true in the most obvious way, yet liberal Christian leaders deny it regularly in an attempt to curry favor with secular science.

The Bible, in Genesis, clearly states that death did not exist in creation until the fall.[8] This is reiterated in the New Testament by the apostle Paul and others.[9] If the earth had been around for billions of years, and hundreds of millions of years had been required for life to reach the level of humankind, then death, suffering, disease, and bloody struggles for existence had not only been around for a long time but were a prerequisite for arrival at the Garden of Eden, which according to this theory stood atop many layers of fossilized remains. So after "creating" man (assumedly using these millions of years of violence to do so), the God of creation called this bloody chaos "very good!" Apparently, on the matters of a perfect creation and death being the wages of sin, the Bible must be wrong.

As a Christian, I have to acknowledge the truth of Dr.

---

[7] G. Bozarth, "The Meaning of Evolution," *American Atheist*, February 1978 19, 30.
[8] Genesis 2:16, 3:19.
[9] Romans 5:12.

What about This, and What about That?

Bozarth's assessment and ask myself, "If the wages of sin are not death, since death predated sin, then what indeed *has* Christ's sacrifice on the cross done for me? From what has He saved me?" The conclusion has to be that on the doctrine of salvation, the Bible would be wrong again.

The same is true of the doctrine of restoration. The Bible clearly declares that one day Christ will return and the earth will be restored to the perfect condition God intended for it. If death and brutal struggle for survival described the "very good" world that was originally created, then we need no such restoration. We have that same world now.

Further, the idea that God used evolution and billions of years to create invalidates most everything that I said in chapter seven. This idea supports a view of God that makes it hard to deny that He is indeed behind evil and suffering in the world. If God's creative methods include death, suffering, bloody competition, catastrophic mass killings and survival of the fittest, then what we see in the world today is just an extension of His methodology and we are justified in being angry at Him and taking little responsibility for our condition on ourselves.

But far more important to the Christian than any of the above is the fact that the Lord Jesus himself accepted these things as true and taught them as historical fact. Joined by Paul, Peter, John and the writer of Hebrews, Jesus reiterated events and characters from the early chapters of Genesis from creation to Abraham. Among a number of examples, Jesus taught on the sanctity of marriage by reference to Genesis 1 and 2,[10] and He said His second advent would be "as it was in the days of Noah."[11] There is no evidence whatsoever that Jesus or His followers understood the creation account to be a literary device

---

[10] Matthew 19:4-6 and Mark 10:6-8.
[11] Matthew 24:37-38.

of any kind. If the Genesis account is not literal history, then Christianity's founders, including God Himself in the form of man, were mistaken and the belief system is chaos.

Profoundly affected by secular opinion, though, evolutionary theologians and theistic philosophers continue to pile up layers of intellectual rescue devices in order to construct a Biblical history that integrates the two opposed viewpoints and avoids having to confront this overwhelmingly marketed error.

Even Dinesh D'Souza, whom I quoted earlier, a brilliant apologist for Christianity in so many ways, shows that his trust and faith in God's Word cannot stand against this tsunami of opinion when he writes,

> "It is important here to clear up a common misunderstanding. Many secular writers seem to think that the orthodox Christian position is that the universe and the earth were literally made in six calendar days. But the Bible uses a Hebrew term that could mean a day or a season or an era."[12]

After reading a good deal of his otherwise excellent book, I was frankly shocked to see this passage. Firstly, the "orthodox" Christian position is to believe what God has clearly revealed to us in scripture. D'Souza cannot claim Christian orthodoxy for an opinion contrary to the plain meaning of the account just because he wishes it to line up

If manipulation of nature by God is a rational possibility, could not the God who spoke matter and natural laws into existence have done so in six seconds?

---

[12] D'Souza, *What's So Great about Christianity.*

What about This, and What about That?

with liberal compromise (which questions secular opinion as little as possible). Secondly, there is, in fact, no difference between the possible meanings of the Hebrew word *Yom*, used in Genesis 1, and the English word *day*. Both can be interpreted in the same possible ways. If the writer had intended for the reader to understand the word as "a season or an era" he could have used other Hebrew words, such as *Olam*, which is used often in the bible to indicate extreme periods of time.

But returning to my point here, D'Souza is far from being the only person who seems able to accept God's omnipotence and ability to manipulate nature at His pleasure, while at the same time, finding the clear statement in Genesis that He created the universe in six calendar days impossible to accept. Why? D'Souza spends several pages in his book defending the belief in miracles as rational. If manipulation of nature by God is a rational possibility, could not the God who spoke matter and natural laws into existence have done so in six seconds? Why is six days so hard to accept? Secular science doesn't accept anything at all that can't be explained naturally, but Christians reject that limitation, understanding that the Entity that established nature with the power of His voice certainly has the option of operating outside of it. So why do we feel so strongly that we have to agree with this one naturalist theory?

Christians should accept that this passage in Genesis 1 that seems to conflict so clearly with the billions-of-years theory and biological evolution *really does conflict with these theories*. If this is the case, then to the Christian, these theories would have to express an incorrect view of reality, because they conflict with truth itself. There is no need to try to re-explain or re-define the rules of language in order to allow for a symbolic, poetic or allegorical[13] meaning to what is clearly a narrative account just to bring it in line with the fallible majority's opinion. This is a misguided attempt to add God's revelation to the conflicting explanation of life that man thinks he has discovered. It reduces a portion of The Truth on which we rely to mythical imagery and places what secular mankind believes above what God has told us. It places human reason above divine revelation—the sin of making oneself the judge of The Creator. The more Christians try to do this, the more the foundation of our faith is weakened. It is my firm conviction that for a Christian, the clear meaning of the Genesis narrative should be enough to inspire a resolved rejection of the idea of Darwinian evolution, the long ages it requires and most of what that entails. Since we accept the Bible as truth, we really need no further explanation.

On the Other Hand...

...it is much more satisfying if the facts and evidence that we find do comport with our beliefs, is it not? Further, as I've pointed out, Christians are compelled by this same Bible to be able to logically support what they believe. Happily, it turns out that there are mountains of strong evidence that geological and biological evolutionary theories are fatally flawed. At the same time, there are many physical evidences that strongly support a young earth and special creation that are virtually always ignored by secular science and the educational system that is driven by it.

The idea of spontaneous chemical reactions giving rise to life is admitted to be beyond the level of impossibility by virtually all scientists, even though most still believe it somehow happened anyway (on one planet or another). And the essential event of one genetic kind of creature changing into another, more

---

[13] Forcing the creation record to imply long eras rather than days wouldn't actually make it symbolism, poetry or allegory. I'm not sure what the name would be of a literary device that tells a specific narrative lie in order to teach a general truth.

complex kind of creature has never been observed, nor is there any known mechanism that would allow it to occur. By way of explanation, the term *species* is a name modern man has given to many morphological (physical appearance) subdivisions of the same kind of creature. Species certainly do change, sometimes amazingly so, as mutations and other genetic and environmental pressures act upon them. Natural selection is an observed process. But natural selection is not evolution. It is frogs changing into different varieties of frogs, and birds to birds, and fruit flies to fruit flies, and bacteria to bacteria. It is not bacteria to fruit flies, or fruit flies to frogs, or frogs to birds. So when someone who sees bacteria mutating and responding differently to antibiotics than they did before claims that evolution is taking place right before their eyes, ask yourself whether or not those bacteria are still bacteria.

Moreover, more and more evidence is being compiled that undermines the assumptions made in evaluating the geological age of the earth. It has been shown that multiple sedimentary rock layers can form in minutes, that under the right circumstances, fossilization does not take more than a few weeks, that coal and even diamonds contain evidence of relative youth, and that sudden, catastrophic events better explain the earth's physical characteristics than slow processes over eons. Likewise, the presence of plutonium radio halos and helium in rocks, together with ridiculously inconsistent age results from the various radiometric dating systems, give good reason to question these methods.

Catastrophic events better explain the Earth's physical characteristics than slow processes over eons.

This area of research is rich with exciting discoveries that support the authority of scripture and help Christians understand better what they should already know: that the Bible contains the unavoidable truth about our reality. Once again, Christian faith is based on reason. Whether you are a Christian or a skeptic, I encourage you to raise your awareness of the research that is available on these subjects.[14] It could change your world view entirely.

Does Attacking Christians Really Discredit Christianity?

When scientific and logical arguments against Christianity begin to fail, there is always the option of attacking what atheists see as its outcomes. If following Christianity results in terrible injustices, interferes with progress and contributes little to society, then it's not even worth looking into as a desirable world view. And if individuals who claim to be Christians often speak, act and think worse than their secular counterparts, who would want to view the belief system as plausible? Richard Dawkins, in his adolescent apology for atheism, *The God Delusion*, rants,

> "Imagine, with John Lennon, a world with no religion. Imagine no suicide bombers, no 9/11, no 7/7, no Crusades, no witch-hunts, no Gunpowder Plot, no Indian partition, no Israeli/Palestinian wars, no Serb/Croat/Muslim massacres, no persecution of Jews as 'Christ-killers', no Northern Ireland 'troubles', no 'honour killings', no shiny-suited bouffant-haired televangelists fleecing gullible people of their money ('God wants you to give till it hurts'). Imagine no Taliban to blow up ancient statues, no public beheadings of blasphemers, no flogging of female skin for the crime of showing an inch of it."[15]

---

[14] A good place to start is www.answersingenesis.com.
[15] Dawkins, *The God Delusion*.

I, along with every authentic Christian, agree with Dawkins that all of the above would be wonderful. But even this seemingly exhaustive list of evils, if all were eliminated, would make little or no dent in the tribulations mankind perpetrates upon itself. Christians often hear objections like, "If so-and-so is a Christian, then no thank you," or "Christians are so intolerant and dogmatic; I don't need that," or "Look at all the evil leaders Christianity has spawned." In other words, Christianity as a belief system, or as a faith, becomes guilty by association with all those who, throughout history, have made bad or evil choices under its banner.

These and other accounts, claims and myths involved in this method of attack on the Christian faith (and other faiths) apply observed effects to the wrong cause. They commit the logical error of "irrelevant thesis." It's true that these things are horrible, but that is irrelevant to the question at issue. The issue is the world view called Christianity, not the actions of the people who call themselves Christian.

There are two points to be made here. Firstly, much of the historical criticism of the Christian church is simply not true or is distorted to support the antagonist viewpoint. Witch-burning, for example, was a phenomenon claimed by many secular historians to have resulted in the deaths of *millions* of women in early-modern Europe. This is an exaggeration still heard in many scholarly settings today, even though recent studies have revised that to thirty or forty thousand. Obviously, there's no question, the practice of hunting down anyone who could remotely fit the description of witch or warlock did, in fact, take place at times in the past, and it resulted in horrible atrocities. It was not always, however, motivated by religious sentiment, and certainly not always by Christians (and never by the teachings of true Christianity).

Along the same lines, the crusades were a reaction to the repeated invasion and harassment of Christian territories over centuries by Muslim armies who were bent on world domination. If ever an offensive was called for, it was certainly during this period. Not unlike the choices free countries face with terrorism today, there comes a time when free people have a right to stand up and deny the advances of those who would oppress them. This truth does not justify the overzealousness and cruelty of many associated with the European crusaders, but it is too convenient to attack Christianity for defending itself against aggression by getting a little too aggressive itself.

Regarding the church attempting to thwart science; it is not true that the early church fiercely resisted things like a spherical earth and heliocentrism. It's true that the idea of the earth being flat was still popular among the uneducated populace for some time after Columbus and Copernicus. But then as now, all one had to do was observe the horizon an a clear day or watch the shadow of the earth against the moon to know that it wasn't flat. The idea that church leadership (on the whole) believed this is a fabrication of modern culture. And the acceptance of the sun as the center of the solar system by the seventeenth-century church was nowhere near the struggle that secular history has made it out to be (though it was certainly resisted by some in the church and some, most famously Galileo, were persecuted for supporting it). It's often ignored that heliocentrism was an idea that was not empirically proven at the time.

Rather than impeding the advance of man's understanding of the physical world, it was the solid foundation of a world view that saw uniformity in the creation of a self-consistent Creator that spurred on modern science. Nearly all of the famous scientists before, during and after the Reformation era either professed Christianity, or at minimum, believed in a Creator God. These included Copernicus, Kepler, Galileo, Bacon, Newton, Pascal, Faraday and on and on, even to the present day.

Finally, the slave trade certainly cannot be placed on the shoulders of Christianity. It's true, of course, that many Christians held slaves in various parts of the world and that many spoke out in its defense, claiming wrongly that it was endorsed in the Bible.[16] But the Christian church did not invent it, and it was the work of Christians that primarily brought about its demise.

The more important point to be made, though, is that this type of argument is a blatant *non sequitur*, as I pointed out in chapter three. It does not follow that Christianity bears responsibility for every folly its defenders carry out. It may have been obvious, in the paragraphs above, that I didn't try to thoroughly document my objections to these claims of critics or to discuss them in much depth. I didn't bother with that because it simply doesn't matter. Many of the indictments of the Christian church's historical actions (such as, most notably, the Spanish Inquisition) or the behaviors of Christian individuals are, in fact, mostly valid, but the degree to which some of them are fabrications or exaggerations really misses the point. If this type of argument is to hold sway, then certainly the Christian could counter with

> *Jesus...was a peaceful man who, rather than enslaving people, sought to set them free.*

---

[16] Just to touch on the claim that slavery was endorsed by first-century Christianity: Much of the slavery one would find in the Palestine of that era was vastly different from that of modern times. It could more properly be described as indentured servitude. Slavery in this context was limited in time (freedom was in the foreseeable future). Most often, a person entered into this relationship voluntarily as a way of paying off debt, and most slaves were treated well, more like modern people would expect household servants to be treated. Whether it was regarding this type of slavery—practiced more by the indigenous peoples—or the crueler, Roman kind, Christ advised all slaves to serve their masters with integrity, urging them to bring respect and dignity to themselves and their circumstances.

mountains of evidence concerning the beneficial effects of Christian philosophy or Christian individuals on all aspects of society, or recite a litany of horrors perpetrated by strictly secular or atheistic leaders and institutions. Pol Pot, Stalin, Hitler, Mao Zedong, and others were atheists who together murdered hundreds of millions. Is it reasonable that those who follow in their atheistic beliefs about reality should indict Christianity for its share of atrocity over the ages?

Jesus himself, who Christians follow as God and Savior, was a peaceful man who, rather than enslaving people, sought to set them free. He respected and elevated women above their lowly station in that day,[17] and the only war he ever launched or endorsed was a spiritual one.

Christians who truly follow the faith they hold dear have been the driving force behind education for everyone, the abolition of slavery, the most important scientific advances, the protection of Jews being persecuted under Hitler, the foundation of democracy, and even the very structure of the world's view of good and evil. Actually, "the whipping of slaves, burning of heretics, pogroms against minorities, and the scandalous personal lives of 'televangelists' become obscene [only] in the light of the gospel."[18] Without the tenets of the Christian faith and the yardstick of good and evil that has been discussed in these pages, how would we even judge these things wrong? This repeated canard that Christianity interferes with progress and contributes little to society is the worst kind of unsupported nonsense. The reality is that for the past two thousand years of history, mankind—Christian and otherwise—has been in the throes of a struggle to measure up to the principles of Christianity. *The trouble with the world is that it*

---

[17] Did you spend any time wondering what the word *day* meant here? I was just wondering.
[18] Marshall, *The Truth Behind the New Atheism.*

is not Christian enough.

Jesus called His followers to be "the light of the world" and "the salt of the earth." Is it reasonable to blame Him for those who do the opposite in His name? Is it a logical progression of thought to say, "I know some bad (stupid, fanatical, hateful, murderous, etc.) people who claim to be Christians, therefore Christianity is bad"? I don't think such a statement would get you on the debate team. Author Ted Kluck put it well when he wrote, "Don't throw the baby out with the bathwater. Don't lump Jesus and the gospel in with the *Left Behind* movies, TBN, Joel Osteen, Joyce Meyer, or whatever else you may be using as your reason to be disillusioned with Christianity."[19]

A Restriction to Freedom?

The underlying criticism behind all of this—the scientific objections, the *ad hominem* attacks, the attempts to connect the evil acts of men and institutions to the belief system of Christianity and so forth—is that the belief in an all-powerful Creator and in the need for redemption and reconciliation through Christ is an imposition and a restriction on man's perceived right to rule himself. We have been taught that we don't have to see ourselves as created by anybody. We are the accidental pinnacle of nature's random activity, and therefore by the right of good luck, we should rule over ourselves and the rest of creation. The basic complaint that underlies all these others is, *God wants to run my life, and I don't want Him to.* It is really as simple as that.

Those who haven't understood Christianity in its totality see it as a restriction to freedom, a set of chains placed on choices and behavior. I understand this reaction because I have felt that

---

[19] K. DeYoung and T. Kluck, *Why We're Not Emergent (By Two Guys Who Should Be)* (Chicago: Moody Publishers, 2008). No disrespect is intended to the persons and entities in Mr. Kluck's example.

same way myself. But I am so grateful to know now that God has made me for a reason. The idea that I might have been a random accident or that if I was in fact created, it was in a way completely contrary to the Bible's account, affected me for decades in ways I haven't yet fully comprehended. I see now how influenced I was by man's idea that to eliminate God is to set himself free—free to run his own life, to make his own decisions, and to decide right and wrong for himself. Although a Christian, I wanted to be "free" like that as well. Like the prodigal son of Luke 15, I was determined to remove myself from the influence and authority of my (heavenly) Father. By our nature, we all are.

So because I, like all others of my species, liked the idea of ruling over my own life, I was seduced by the kind of teaching that we all receive in our schools. In my humanness, I began to accept the "facts" that everyone insisted had been proved, and so my faith remained weak. Why wouldn't it? I was hearing things taught that were contrary to it every day. Science was behind these things, I was told, so how could an ordinary man disagree? All my friends and acquaintances were taught these same things and most, even the Christians, seemed to believe them. I lived in a world that believed God had been proved irrelevant to my physical existence and there didn't seem to be any solid refutation of that idea forthcoming from my Christian mentors, who often seemed as flawed as any heathen I knew.

But through the years, as I tried to run my own life, I eventually learned, mistake by painful mistake, that I was not very good at it. Most honest people find the same thing. As I approached midlife I saw that my best effort at running my own life had left me confused and unsure, like a broken-masted schooner adrift at sea. I could look back only on a trail of ruined relationships and the ill effects of an undirected life on those I had loved most. My life had sometimes brought me happiness, but there had never been the underlying joy and fulfillment that come from understanding. Ultimately, I had no comprehension of why in the world I even existed. Just like that ungrateful son Jesus described to the Pharisees in the Prodigal Son parable, I found that freedom of that kind, once I had it, wasn't what I anticipated. Instead of the wonderful liberation that running things for myself was supposed to produce, I found that the chains I heard clinking were not those of my Christian faith but those placed on me over the decades by my counterfeit gods; financial gain, personal enjoyment, success and self-rule. But even I, as a member of the most advanced species known to exist, couldn't figure out how to free myself from the disappointment and confusion I faced every day. I had lost all hope of ever achieving the fulfillment that my inner being taught me to crave. I didn't understand that to serve these forms of human gratification above the God I knew was to be a slave to them. I didn't know I was chained up behind the great door of N. T. Wright's "prison in the cosmos."[20]

Finally, I came to the point of asking myself this logical progression of questions. These represent the crux of all that has been discussed herein:

- *Is it in my best interest to depend upon myself and others of my species to explain and direct my life?*
- *If not, do I have a choice? Is there another person or entity upon whom I can lean for understanding and direction in creating the best life I can experience while here in this fallen world?*
- *And if there is, what does that mean for my future?*

Every person who cares about discovering the true character of his or her reality must answer these questions. If you ignore

---

[20] See the closing paragraphs of chapter eight.

them, you will never be free of the chains of hopelessness. I can only say for myself that to know with confidence, based on logic and good evidence, that I am a child of the Creator God, and that He wishes to relate personally to me is more freeing a notion than any I have ever heard suggested. I relate completely to the attitude of Chris Tomlin, a musician who seems to understand that as it turns out, real freedom is found in a relationship with the One who knows it all and loves us without condition, when he sings:

> *"My chains are gone; I've been set free,*
> *My God, my Savior, has ransomed me,*
> *And like a flood His mercy reigns,*
> *Unending love, amazing grace!"* [21]

For the Christian, fulfillment comes from attaching ourselves to One who doesn't make these mistakes that we humans can never seem to avoid. He is correct in all He says and does, morally, scientifically, socially, historically, politically and in every way. In Him, we never stumble or err, so we are perfectly happy and fulfilled. It is only when we stray from our relationship with Him and lean on our own understanding (a daily occurrence for most of us) that we fall back into error and lose that fulfillment.

Charlie Brown, in the opening quote of this chapter, was certainly right. Figuring out the essence of our reality definitely takes more than one night. Many never even try. For a long time, I didn't, partly because it was complicated, partly because I didn't know where to find answers, but mostly because I just didn't want to. But the questions kept nagging, the inborn need

---

[21] J. Newton, J. Rees, C. Tomlin, E. Excell, L. Giglio et al., "Amazing Grace (My Chains Are Gone)" (New York: EMI Christian Music Group, 2006).

to know kept prodding and the drive for personal fulfillment kept motivating. Eventually I knew I had to try.

We all have that need, placed in us by our Creator, whether we're ready to answer it or not. In the introduction to this book, I asked the skeptical seeker to step back for a while from doubts, put on hold the many criticisms that are out there about Christianity and plan to pick them up again after reading. If this describes you and you are still reading, you are indeed a seeker of truth, whether you have bought into anything you've read here or not. If you keep this up, you will get to the truth because God has created you in a way that will get you there. Surely none of us will ever figure out every detail, but if we continually put our amazing minds to the task, we can get to the point where we *"see through a glass darkly"*[22] at least. Putting aside prejudice, and all the noise of the culture and the agenda of those whose highest goal is to justify their arrogance, it is hard not to believe. Our Creator has assured us that we can't help but get there if we just keep thinking!

---

[22] A phrase coined by the apostle Paul in I Corinthians 13:12.

Appendix

The Christian World View

After reading this book, a reader would be justified in wondering just what version of Christianity it endorses. Obviously, hundreds of millions of people all over the globe call themselves Christian, and among them one would find scores of variations in interpretation and conviction regarding different questions of faith. So how could one author claim to authoritatively know the correct "Christian world view?" Individual denominations vary greatly in theological and practical interpretation of scripture, areas of emphasis, philosophical points of view, worship practices, reliance on tradition, view of history and so forth. *Most often* though, these areas of disagreement relate to the fleshing out, if you will, of worship, the relative importance of peripheral issues and how to best live out the Christian life. This is not to say that these things are not important (some are critically important), but they are *usually* issues that are distant to some degree from the core tenets of the Christian faith. Rather than being the nuclear assumptions that drive the way one looks at the world, they are expressions of those assumptions. Many influences direct how one lives out his world view, and humans, being the complex

Appendix A

creatures they are, don't always act consistently with it.

One reason that this book is subtitled *A Personal Christian Manifesto* is that it is meant to be no more than one person's view and therefore should not be looked at as an expression of some particular denomination's doctrine. It is only one person's plea for the reader to see that Christianity, at its heart, is a call to understand and interpret the world in the way that God has explained it to us in scripture. Putting aside pride and the desire for intellectual autonomy, Christians are required by scripture to bring their thinking under the authority of their Creator.[1] *We are expected to understand and continuously keep a grip on the simple and obvious fact that God is the Creator and we are the created.* If we truly believe and internalize this simple truth, we will never elevate human thinking above the declarations of the omniscient God. As fallible creatures, Christians will certainly disagree, argue and even fight over many issues. We, like all others, do that because our knowledge and understanding are not perfect in this time and place and because our personalities and points of view vary from person to person.

With that mind, I submit the following core elements of an authentic Christian world view. In order to be Christian, a person's world view must include the following and contain nothing that conflicts with it:

God is a spiritual, or supernatural, being who exists outside of time. He is the only self-existent, logically necessary, uncreated being. He is not bound by chronological thinking, as we are, because the whole concept of time was His idea. God's creativity and power are the source of everything that we know, with the exception of evil, which is the expression of rebellion in His created beings. As the Imaginer, Creator and Sustainer of every

---

[1] See Romans 12:2, II Corinthians 10:5.

aspect of our reality, He is rightfully the Owner of it. As the One who established reality and set its parameters, He is, by definition, correct and just in everything He says and does within that reality. The idea that God could be "wrong" in any sense is not a possibility in the Christian world view. While God is the owner and master of all that He created, it is important to understand the *reason* that He created. God's nature is love. He perfectly exemplifies real love as described in I Corinthians 13 and throughout scripture. Real love must express itself, and the reason for our existence and that of the entire cosmos in which we live is to provide a place into which God's overwhelming love can flow.

God is a triune being consisting of three separate but completely unified personalities. These personalities operate in perfect accord because they all have the same perfect understanding of the physical and spiritual worlds, and the same purpose and will. This is an attribute of their common nature. They are, in fact, one being: God. For reasons beyond the scope of this document, we differentiate these personalities from one another by referring to them as The Father, The Son, and The Holy Spirit.

Jesus Christ is the name of an historical person who was for a time the *incarnate* (endowed with a human physical body) member of this unified Godhead. This God personality existed in human form in order to teach mankind how to live successfully and to take upon Himself (God) the just penalty for the sin of His creation. In this way, Jesus provided a way for man to reconcile himself to the God from whom he was estranged because of sin. Jesus was and is a coequal member of the Trinity, and during His time in the physical world, He was fully God and fully man. He was also a full participating partner in creation and now exists both outside of nature and within it, as He always has.

As a sinless man, Jesus Christ not only suffered the physical consequences of man's sin by allowing Himself to be crucified, but He also conquered them forever by not staying dead. His bodily resurrection, together with our free choice to accept its gift of salvation, are the critical keys to our redemption.

The Bible is the inspired word of the Creator God. It is the only completely reliable written history available to mankind. God gave it to His created ones in order that they could understand Him and His creation correctly. God has preserved and protected His word from loss and error so that all mankind can benefit from it. It is to be understood according to the normal use of language with an understanding of the cultural and linguistic environment in which it was given. It is the standard by which Christians measure truth.

Given these truths, a Christian should view his world in this way:

All knowledge and understanding of reality come from God. God is the source of the entire system of thinking and reason that we have, called logic. Because we are created in His image, we think much like He does, though subject to human limitations. If the source of any understanding that man has about reality is not God, then it is *subject to* being in error, no matter how brilliantly it is defended or how widely it is believed. If it contradicts anything that God has specifically told us, then it is, by definition, incorrect. Created beings cannot discover truths contradictory to those given by their Creator because none exist.

God has implanted in us at birth certain attributes and understandings about reality:

1) <u>A logical perspective</u>. Our minds are orderly, like God's. We embrace first-principals such as non-contradiction, cause and effect and so forth. Based on these, we cherish deductive reasoning as well as strong inductive

reasoning. We renounce hypotheses that stray too far from these principals.
2) <u>The ability to draw inferences from observation</u>. From what we see, we know that there must be a Creator who began all things. Because of the gift of orderly thinking, we are confident in drawing conclusions from observing the physical world, while always respecting and affirming the authority of scripture.
3) <u>The realization that objective good, evil, right and wrong exist in the world</u>. Again, our orderly minds tell us that ethics (our secular term for right, wrong, good and evil) exist as a system of behavior that is objectively correct. That is, the most important ethical behavior cannot be defined by any human or society. If it were defined that way, then all ethics would be relative, and no one would have any basis on which to judge any behavior objectively right or wrong. However, objective ethics do exist, and they derive from the character of a Law Giver outside of humanity who we are programmed to emulate. This Law Giver is God.

Humankind is made in the image of God. Therefore, every living person is highly valuable and overflowing with potential. Mankind is a spiritual being made to exist permanently but is animated in the physical world with a temporary body. He is made to find his highest fulfillment in knowing, glorifying, sharing and worshiping his Creator.

The relationship between God and man is severed by sin. God is holy, or perfect, by nature, so He cannot coexist with error. In order to repair this relationship, man must realize his error and helplessness, freely choose to accept the work of Christ on the cross and in the resurrection, and acknowledge

Appendix A

openly and verbally that he is a follower of Christ.[2]

These are the perspectives and presuppositions from which every Christian should be viewing his world, considering the thoughts and ideas he encounters, and beginning his reasoning in every area of life.

---

[2] See Romans 10:9&10.

Suggested Reading

Current research and philosophy from a Christian perspective regarding:

The Absolute Nature of Truth and Its Independence from Culture

- *Total Truth,* Nancy Pearcey and Phillip Johnson
- *The Truth War,* John MacArthur, Jr.

Evidence for the Genesis Flood and Rapid Stratification

- *The Earth's Catastrophic Past,* Andrew Snelling
- *The Geological Column: Perspectives within Diluvial Geology,* John Reed and Michael Oard
- *Studies in Flood Geology,* John Woodmorappe
- http://www.globalflood.org
- *The Grand Canyon: Monument to the Flood,* Institute for Creation Research

Suggested Reading

Radiometric Dating/Age of the Earth and Universe

- *The Young Earth: The Real History of the Earth—Past, Present, and Future*, John Morris
- *Radioisotopes and the Age of the Earth, Volumes I and II*, Larry Vardiman, Andrew Snelling and Eugene Chaffin
- *The Mythology of Modern Dating Methods*, John Woodmorappe
- *Coming to Grips with Genesis*, Terry Mortenson and Thane Ury

The Ice Age

- *An Ice Age Caused by the Genesis Flood*, Michael Oard
- *Ancient Ice Ages or Gigantic Submarine Landslides?*, Michael Oard

Reasons to Accept the Biblical Record of Creation

- *In Six Days; Why 50 Scientists Choose to Believe in Creation*, John F. Ashton
- *The Battle for the Beginning*, John MacArthur, Jr.
- *The Ultimate Proof of Creation*, Jason Lisle
- *Not a Chance*, R. C. Sproul

World View, Atheism vs. Christianity

- *War of the Worldviews*, Ken Ham, Bodie Hodge, Karl Kerby, Jason Lisle, Stacia McKeever, David Menton, Terry Mortenson, Georgia Purdom and Mike Riddle
- *How Should We Then Live*, Francis Schaeffer

- *I Don't Have Enough Faith to Be an Atheist*, Norman Geisler and Frank Turek**
- *Reasonable Faith: Christian Truth and Apologetics*, William Lane Craig
- *What's So Great about Christianity*, Dinesh D'Souza **
- *The Truth Behind the New Atheism*, David Marshall **
- *The Big Argument: Does God Exist*, John Ashton and Michael Westacott, compilers

Problems with the Theory of Evolution

- *Evolution: A Theory in Crisis*, Michael Denton
- *The Lie: Evolution*, Ken Ham
- *Darwin on Trial*, Phillip Johnson
- *The New Answers Book*, *The New Answers Book 2* and *The New Answers Book 3*, Ken Ham, editor
- *Bones of Contention*, Marvin Lubinow
- www.answersingenesis.org
- www.trueorigin.org
- www.icr.org/ICR-Resources

Intelligent Design

- *Darwin's Black Box: The Biochemical Challenge to Evolution*, Michael Behe[Δ]
- *The Design Revolution: Answering the Toughest Questions About Intelligent Design*, William Dembski[Δ]

Suggested Reading

Problems with Integrating Evolution with Christianity

- *Did God Use Evolution?*, Werner Gitt
- *Old-Earth Creationism on Trial*, Tim Chaffey and Jason Lisle

The Reliability of the Bible and the Validity of Christ's Claim to be God

- *The New Evidence That Demands a Verdict*, Josh McDowell
- *Conspiracies and the Cross*, Timothy Paul Jones
- *The Case for Faith*, and *The Case for Christ*, Lee Strobel
- *The Reason for God*, Timothy Keller **

The Christian View of Spirituality and the Afterlife

- *Heaven and the Afterlife*, James Garlow and Keith Wall

** Although the resources tagged with stars contain powerful arguments for faith in a Creator, they also contain an acceptance of the secular dogma of an extreme age of the earth and universe with which this author does not agree. I believe such a belief critically weakens these authors' cases.

Δ Intelligent Design, as a movement, presents powerful arguments for a super intelligent designer but makes no claims as to who the designer may be, thus supporting no particular faith or philosophy's understanding of Him. While these and other authors' logic regarding design is inescapable, they do not help the reader reason out the next logical question—namely, "Who is this designer?"

Acknowledgements

I'm so grateful for the encouragement of friends and family in this long and satisfying effort. I'd like to thank my friends, Dr. Charles Joiner, the most accomplished businessman, Christian leader, and family man I know, and Reverend Dave Blackburn, who models friendship and integrity in a way I can only dream of emulating; my big brother, Dr. Fred Wilson, to whom I still look for wisdom and affirmation; and my wife, Debbie, a timeless beauty from any perspective, who all gave up many hours of their valuable time reading the manuscript and offering me input and advice aimed at making the work as good as it could be. The high quality of these peoples' lives arises from their understanding of the truths repeated in this work. The kind of help they freely gave is invaluable to any author, and I'm thankful for their expertise, their input and their enthusiasm.

For authors, ideas come from all kinds of often unexpected sources. As I indicate in the introduction, this one came from a very special man who I have pseudonymed "James" in order to protect his privacy. Without his piercing observations, accusations and points of view, this book would never have come to be. I thank him for that.

And of course, I will always be grateful to those who have

Acknowledgements

supported my work by making comments, introducing me to others who could be helpful and generally cheering me on.

Finally, I have to acknowledge the true source of the world view presented in this book. The God presented to the reader herein, through creation, His word and the gift of reason, has offered truth to anyone who will open themselves to it. Through my parents, teachers, pastors, family, friends and a lifetime of experiences, choices and consequences, both negative and positive, I came to accept this truth. This book is another step along the fantastic journey of expanding, internalizing and fully knowing it.

> *…Jesus commands my destiny.*
> *No power of hell, no scheme of man can ever pluck me from His hand,*
> *Till He returns, or calls me home, here in the power of Christ I'll stand.*[1]

---

[1] S. Townend and K. Getty, "In Christ Alone" (Eastbourne, UK: Kingsway/Thankyou Music, 2001).

About the Author

Donald R. Wilson has enjoyed a career as a pilot of luxury private jets serving large corporations and very wealthy individuals in worldwide operations. His thirty-seven years of traveling the globe have given him a unique perspective on our world and its people. Donald holds a degree in Professional Aeronautics from Embry-Riddle University and has served in a number of leadership and training positions during his career. Always interested in writing, he has published a number of articles in various aviation publications and written on family issues for *Home Life* and *Parenting*.

Some years ago, Donald became interested in the underlying evidence and logic for his lifelong faith in a Creator God. In studying and considering this issue, he realized that Christianity, indeed faith in God in general, could not stand unless its key claims, when dissected under the brightest-possible light of scientific, philosophical and logical scrutiny and without bias or presupposition, were found to be credible. This journey has confirmed for Donald the amazing truth that the Creator God is real, that He can be shown to exist through logic alone if need be and that the Biblical claims that He created all that exists in our reality in flashes of power and brilliance beyond anything we can imagine are true in the most authentic sense of the word. Further, the histories presented in the Bible, the claims of Christ

About the Author

and His disciples, and the Christian teachings about life and the future provide a complete understanding of the real nature of our existence.

Several years of talking with people of all points of view and backgrounds convinced Donald that there are too few people—from atheists to religious zealots—that sufficiently grasp the issues required for a clear understanding of reality. People are interested and searching, but in our society there is nearly nowhere to turn for a clear, unified presentation of what is real and how we know it. This debut work is Donald's way of contributing to the righting of the listing ship of world view that characterizes so many people's perception of life.

Donald resides in the southeastern United States with his wife, Debbie.